*"A map is the greatest of all epic poems.
Its lines and colors show the realization
of great dreams."*

Gilbert Grosvenor, Editor, National Geographic, 1903–1954

The maps in this book are created with GIS technology and reflect the visions and dreams of users. Each map tells a story, often an epic story, of some aspect of our world. By telling the story and sharing it we can see how dreams are realized.

Some maps involve integration of data for scientific modeling and knowledge creation. Some focus on the creation of information for planning and decision making. Others simply communicate complicated studies to coworkers and the public. Examples of these and others are included in this book.

1999 is the International Year of the Ocean, and to commemorate it we have also included several fine examples of ocean maps showing features such as currents, bathymetry, and maritime boundaries.

With the growth of mapping and GIS on the Internet, the world of map creation and geographic knowledge dissemination will greatly expand. GIS users are learning this new medium and will leverage their efforts, resulting in an enormous leap in geographic literacy. GIS maps will play an important role in the information society as they help us better understand our reality and organize our knowledge for many beneficial activities.

My colleagues and I would like to thank all the users who allowed ESRI to publish their maps in this book. We applaud their efforts and eagerly look forward to seeing the maps that they and other users create in the coming year.

Warm regards,

Jack Dangermond

Planning Wisconsin — Remaining Farmland in Dane County

Agriculture

Land Information and Computer Graphics Facility, University of Wisconsin, Madison, Wisconsin

By Todd Sutphin, Math Heinzel, and Doug Miskowiak

Contact:
Tom McClintock
tlmcclin@facstaff.wisc.edu

Software:
ARC/INFO Version 7.1.2 and ArcView GIS Version 3.0a
Hardware:
Sun workstation and Pentium II 266
Plotter:
Hewlett–Packard DesignJet 2500
Data Source(s):
USGS Digital Line Graphs, Dane County Land Information Office, Dane County soil survey, 1995 census boundaries, and 1995 digital elevation model

This map shows the distribution of soils in Dane County, Wisconsin, classified by soil grade. The grades are assigned by the Department of Revenue (DOR) as a measure of productivity for assessment purposes. DOR Grade 1 soils are the most productive, while Grade 3 soils are the least productive.

Overlaid on the soil coverage are municipal areas as well as other land use classifications including residential, mercantile, industrial, and rural urbanizing patterns, which are not available for farming.

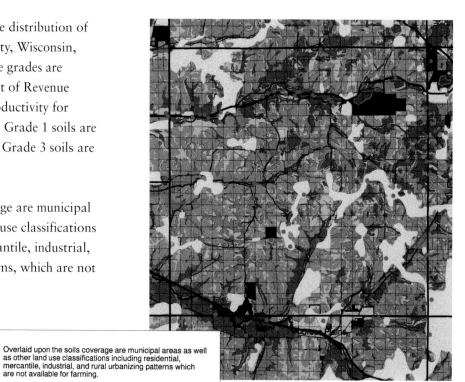

Overlaid upon the soils coverage are municipal areas as well as other land use classifications including residential, mercantile, industrial, and rural urbanizing patterns which are not available for farming.

- • Farm Unit
- Rural Urbanizing Patterns
- Townships
- Railroad Right-of-way
- Highways
- Madison Streets
- County Parcels
- Rivers and Streams
- Lakes
- 200' buffer - Slow/No Wake Zone
- 75' buffer around streams and lakes
- Residential
- Public and Protected Ownership
- Mercantile tax class
- Industrial tax class
- Wetlands
- Steep slopes over 12%
- 1995 Census Municipal Boundaries
- Municipalities
- Missing Data

Dorsoil Grade	Total acres in each Grade	Remaining soils in each Grade	Percent of Total
1	320,987	177,220	55.2%
2	232,032	130,458	56.2%
3	214,394	88,428	41.2%

Data Sources:

Streams, lakes, and highways from 1:100,000-scale Digital Line Graphs, originally from USGS.

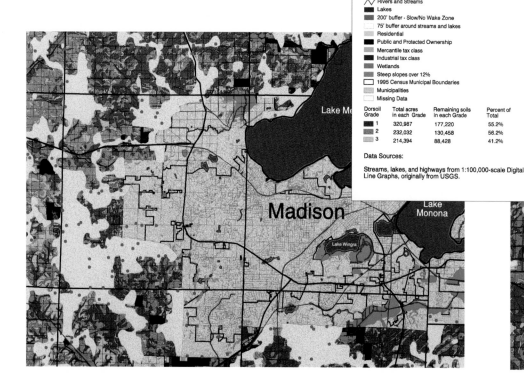

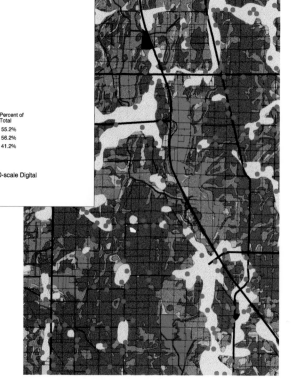

GIS: A Research-Support Tool for the Sugarcane Crop

Centro de Investigacion de la Cana de Azucar de Colombia – CENICANA, Bogota, Colombia

By J. Carbonell and B.V. Ortiz

Contact:
J. Carbonell
jacarbon@cenicana.org

Software:
ArcView GIS Version 3.0a, ArcView Spatial Analyst, and ArcCAD Version 11.3
Hardware:
Compaq 4000 and CalComp digitizing tablet
Plotter:
Hewlett–Packard 755CM
Data Source(s):
Automated Meteorological Network (AMN) and IGAC soil studies

One of the main concerns of the Colombian Sugarcane Research Center, CENICANA, is to determine which variables have an impact on production. The geographic information system (GIS) has contributed notably to the research projects and decision making with respect to the sugarcane crop in the geographic valley of the Cauca River. These projects illustrate the use of GIS in three research projects: the integration of climatic variables for establishing climatic groups; the inclusion of a semi-detailed study of soils for the entire geographic valley and the products derived from this information through GIS; and the generation of thematic productivity maps, which facilitate the interpretation of the complex temporal and spatial variability inherent in it.

Cane-growing potential area of the Cauca river geographic valley (385.000 Has)

The basic data for the projects were rainfall and radiation for the period 1994–1997, originating from the 13 meteorological stations located throughout the geographic valley of the Cauca River and belonging to the automated meteorological network (AMN) of the Colombian sugarcane network, as well as production data from the Cauca, Central Castilla, La Cabana, Providencia, Pichichi, and Riopaila mills covering 131.421 hectares.

The use of GIS facilitates analysis of data from different sources. Data from the AMN, the commercial production of the sugar mills, and soils studies such as the one carried out by the IGAC generates results that provide support not only to CENICANA researchers as a source of information in their projects but also to the sugarcane sector so that they can make appropriate decisions.

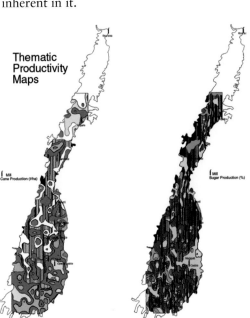

Thematic Productivity Maps

Mill Cane Production (t/ha)

Mill Sugar Production (%)

Solar Radiation (1994-1997)

Met. Station (cal/cm2)*day

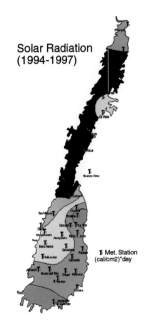

Rainfall (1994-1997)

Met. Station Rainfall (mm/year)

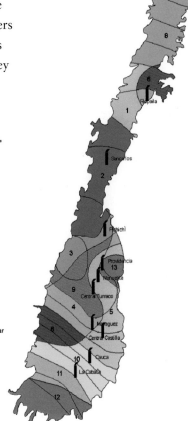

World Map of Natural Hazards

Munich Reinsurance Company,
Munich, Germany

*By Munich Re's Geoscience
Research Group*

Contact:
Andreas Siebert
asiebert@munichre.com

Software:
ARC/INFO Version 7.1 and
ArcView GIS Version 3.0
Hardware:
Windows NT and Pentium 200
Plotter:
Printed
Data Source(s):
Worldwide information on natural
hazards and catastrophes

This map provides information about exposure to windstorms, earthquakes, storm surges, hail, lightning strikes, and other natural events around the world. It can be used as an aid in risk management for insurance purposes, catastrophe preparedness, and public planning projects.

The first edition of the World Map of Natural Hazards was presented by Munich Re's geoscientists 20 years ago. This synopsis of natural hazards has now been entirely revised, incorporating all of the latest scientific data and state-of-the-art techniques such as satellite data and risk analysis programs. In order to present this broad spectrum of knowledge, four auxiliary maps have been added to the main map.

In this third edition, all the basic data has been recorded, adjusted, and analyzed with GIS. The maps derived from this data were produced exclusively with the techniques of digital cartography. The latest scientific data can be incorporated into the content at a much faster rate with this method.

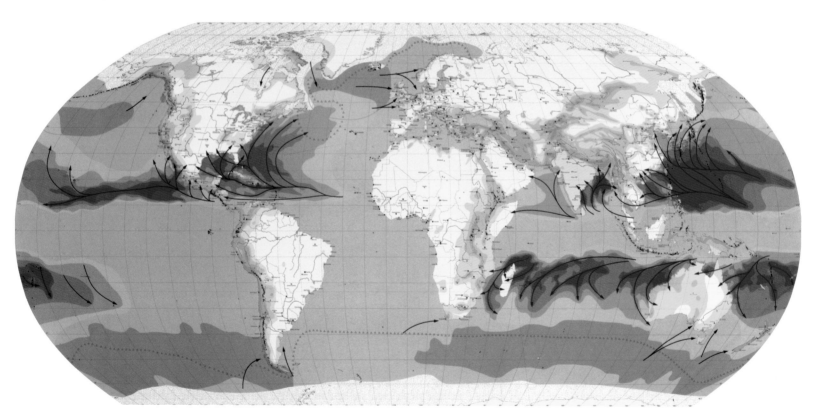

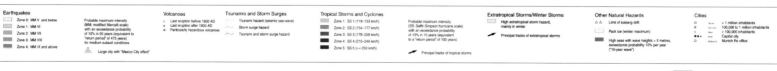

Münchener Rück
Munich Re

A publication accompanying the World Map of Natural Hazards discusses relevant underwriting aspects and presents a comprehensive history of natural catastrophes around the world. The events are broken down by continent and presented in chronological order, with additional information, such as the number of fatalities, and, wherever possible, the economic losses. The locations and distribution of the catastrophic events are also presented on continental maps.

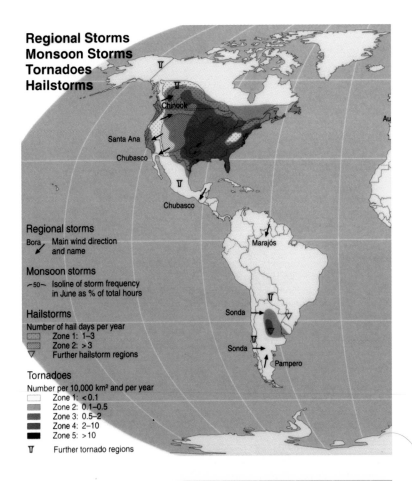

Regional Storms
Monsoon Storms
Tornadoes
Hailstorms

Regional storms
Bora — Main wind direction and name

Monsoon storms
~50~ Isoline of storm frequency in June as % of total hours

Hailstorms
Number of hail days per year
Zone 1: 1–3
Zone 2: >3
▽ Further hailstorm regions

Tornadoes
Number per 10,000 km² and per year
Zone 1: <0.1
Zone 2: 0.1–0.5
Zone 3: 0.5–2
Zone 4: 2–10
Zone 5: >10
☊ Further tornado regions

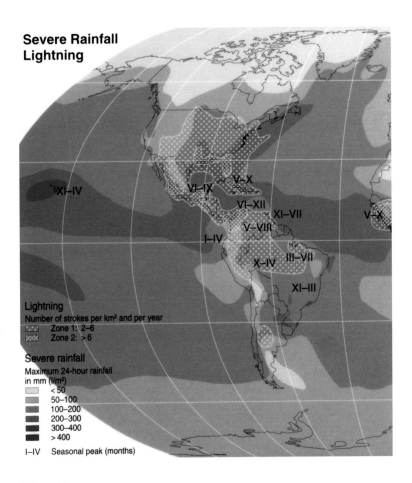

Severe Rainfall
Lightning

Lightning
Number of strokes per km² and per year
Zone 1: 2–6
Zone 2: >6

Severe rainfall
Maximum 24-hour rainfall in mm (l/m²)
< 50
50–100
100–200
200–300
300–400
> 400

I–IV Seasonal peak (months)

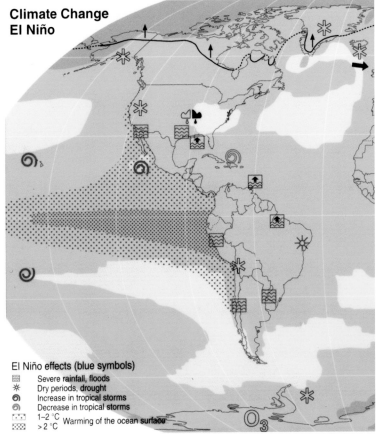

Climate Change
El Niño

El Niño effects (blue symbols)
▨ Severe rainfall, floods
✳ Dry periods, drought
◉ Increase in tropical storms
◉ Decrease in tropical storms
1–2 °C
>2 °C Warming of the ocean surface

3-D Maps Using the Anaglyph Technique

U.S. Army Corps of Engineers,
Topographic Engineering Center,
Alexandria, Virginia

By Todd Blyler

Contact:
Todd Blyler
toddb@tec.army.mil

Software:
ARC/INFO Version 7.1.1
Hardware:
Sun SPARCstation 20
Plotter:
Hewlett–Packard DesignJet 650C
Data Source(s):
USGS and digital elevation
model

These maps demonstrate a methodology for viewing maps and images in three dimensions. To view something in stereo, two concurrent views of the same object are required. The views contain a geometric displacement that permits triangulation. Our brains perform this with the images received by our two eyes, giving us depth perception.

Introducing this parallax to one or more of the red, green, or blue image bands can produce color three-dimensional images. Orthographic digital images can be reorganized to emulate a stereo pair of images. Pixels are shifted along the eye-base varying amounts as a function of the underlying terrain elevation.

The color bands are then recombined to reconstruct the color image. The resultant image is blurry to the naked eye. By using three-dimensional viewing glasses with red and blue color filters, the eyes see only one image at a time. The brain fuses these images together to create color and depth.

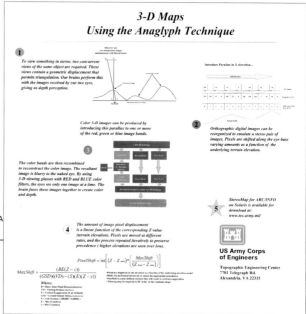

The amount of image pixel displacement is a linear function of the corresponding Z value (terrain elevation). Pixels are moved at different rates, and the process is repeated iteratively to preserve precedence (high elevations are seen over low).

The StereoMap software is available for download at www.tec.army.mil.

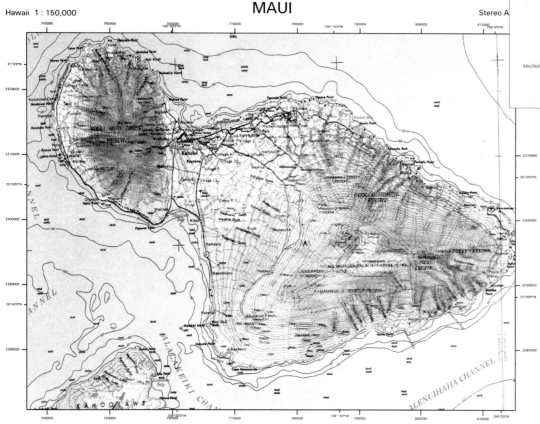

MAUI

Vallentuna Municipality Map

Vallentuna Municipality, Sweden

By T-Kartor Sweden AB,
Inna Nogeste

Contact:
Inna Nogeste
in@t-kartor.se

Software:
ARC/INFO
Plotter:
Printed
Data Source(s):
Proprietary

T-Kartor Sweden AB produced this map with data supplied by the Vallentuna Municipality. The map is used by tourists and for promoting the Vallentuna municipal region.

On one side of the two-sided map is a street map overlaid on a topographic background that features the entire municipality with detailed enlargements of the town center and other sections. The other side includes a vicinity and regional map. There are also photographs of the area's special attractions with descriptions. Information about public transportation, public buildings, recreational areas, and parking is also provided.

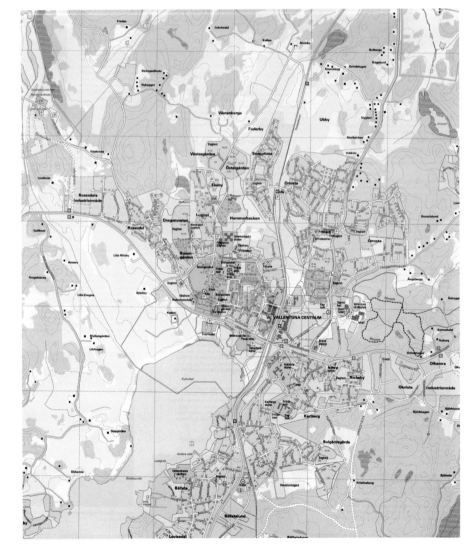

METRO (Method for Elimination of Tilt and Relief Displacement in Orthophotography)

Analytical Surveys, Inc.,
Colorado Springs, Colorado

*By Kevin Trujillo and
Brad Barnell*

Contact:
Kevin Trujillo
ktrujillo@asi-tech.com

Software:
ArcView 3D Analyst
Hardware:
Dell 410 NT workstation
Plotter:
Colorspan 5100 DisplayMaker
Data Source(s):
NYDZP

The images on this poster illustrate a new orthophotography process called METRO that was developed by ASI Technologies.

The main image was created by draping a color orthophoto over a highly detailed TIN using ArcView 3D Analyst. Three-dimensional models were made for several areas of lower Manhattan, including the Wall Street financial district, as part of a pilot project for the New York City Department of Environmental Protection. Color orthophotography and planimetric information were also compiled for all five boroughs of the city.

METRO was developed to produce undistorted orthophotography for aboveground features such as the extremely tall buildings of New York City. In addition, the software fills in the "blind spots" on the ground around buildings or bridges using adjacent photographs of the area. This is important because it enables users of the data to "fly around" a tall building and view or analyze ground features on all four sides of the building.

Highly Detailed TIN

Blind-Spot Elimination

True 3D Polygons

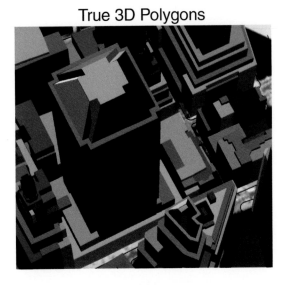

Orthorectified Bridges

Extruded Buildings

Underground Facilities

A Rapid Assessment of Tiger Conservation Units Across Asia:
Tiger Conservation Units and Remaining Vegetation (Indian Subcontinent Bioregion)

Conservation Science Program,
World Wildlife Fund,
Washington, D.C.

*By Prashant Hedao and
Melissa Connor*

Contact:
David Olson
david.olson@wwfus.org

Software:
ARC/INFO Version 7.1.2
Hardware:
Hewlett–Packard UNIX
workstations
Plotter:
Hewlett–Packard 650C and
755CM
Data Source(s):
Asian Bureau for Conservation
and the World Monitoring Centre

This map shows the distribution and extent of tiger habitat types and Tiger Conservation Units (TCUs) in the Indian Subcontinent bioregion. Similar maps were prepared for the Indochina, Southeast Asia, South China, and Russian Far East bioregions. Each bioregion was divided into tiger habitat types, which represent major habitat types where tigers are known to play distinct ecological roles and are members of distinct ecological communities. Conserving examples of tiger populations in distinct bioregions, ecosystems, and habitat types meets a fundamental goal of conservation biology—maintaining representation—while

TCUs are blocks or clusters of blocks of existing habitats that contain, or have the potential to contain, interacting populations of tigers. A TCU can consist of several adjacent blocks of habitat among which tigers can disperse. Adjacent habitats are considered to comprise a TCU if they are linked by degraded scrub forests, tall crops, plantations with dense growth or canopy cover, or river and stream courses. Tigers can disperse across these altered habitats or along river courses.

Adjacent habitat blocks are also considered TCUs if they are separated by less than five kilometers. Field studies in India indicate that five kilometers is approximately the threshold of open land that tigers will cross. Habitat blocks separated by more than five kilometers of open land were delineated as distinct TCUs. Also, TCUs are not restricted to nor contain protected areas, but instead include the entire landscape of natural habitats over which tigers may disperse and become established.

Further analysis of this map included scoring the TCUs for conservation potential based on habitat integrity, poaching pressure, and population status. The TCUs were then ranked in categories representing high, medium, and low probability for persistence of tigers. Comparison of TCUs within bioregional and tiger habitat groupings allowed a representative assessment of tiger habitat areas and a representative prioritization of conservation efforts.

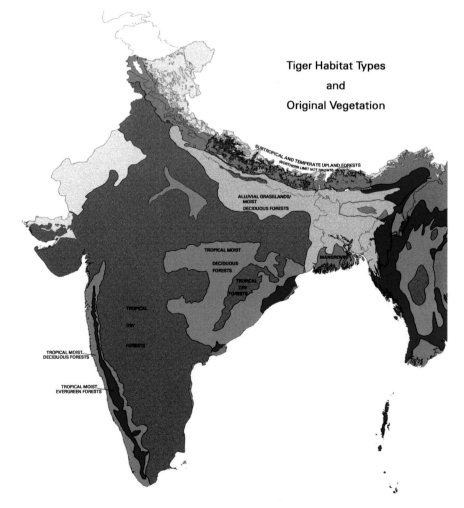

**Tiger Habitat Types
and
Original Vegetation**

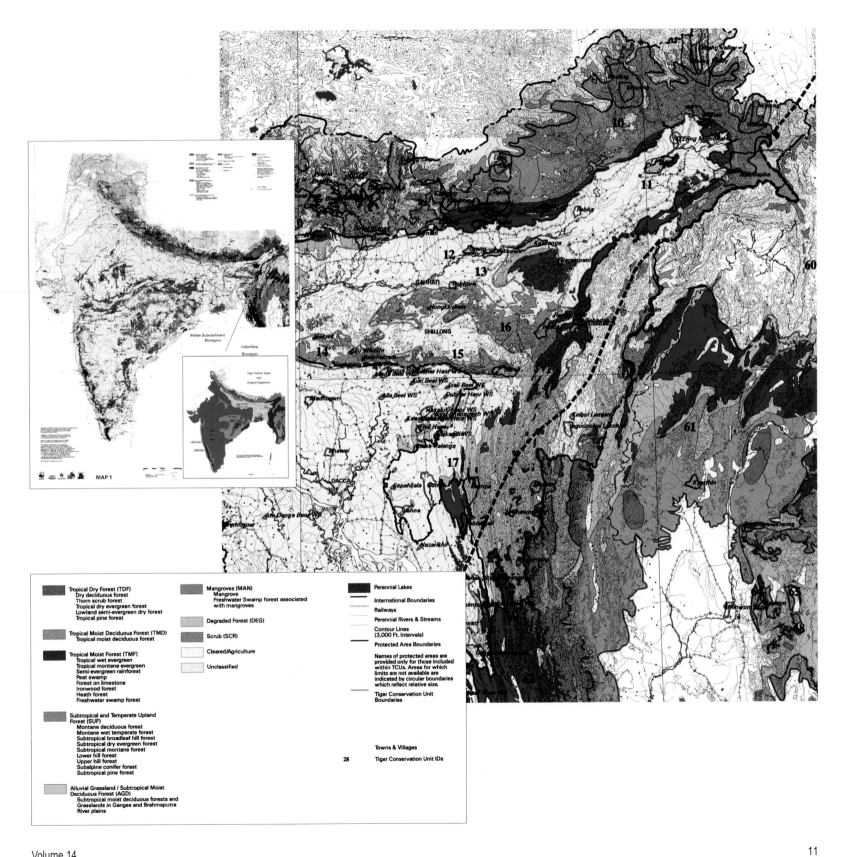

MAP 1

Indian Subcontinent
Bioregion

Indochina
Bioregion

Tiger Habitat Types
and
Original Vegetation

Tropical Dry Forest (TDF)	Mangroves (MAN)	Perennial Lakes
Dry deciduous forest	Mangrove	International Boundaries
Thorn scrub forest	Freshwater Swamp forest associated	Railways
Tropical dry evergreen forest	with mangroves	Perennial Rivers & Streams
Lowland semi-evergreen dry forest		Contour Lines
Tropical pine forest	Degraded Forest (DEG)	(3,000 Ft. Intervals)

Tropical Dry Forest (TDF)
Dry deciduous forest
Thorn scrub forest
Tropical dry evergreen forest
Lowland semi-evergreen dry forest
Tropical pine forest

Tropical Moist Deciduous Forest (TMD)
Tropical moist deciduous forest

Tropical Moist Forest (TMF)
Tropical wet evergreen
Tropical montane evergreen
Semi-evergreen rainforest
Peat swamp
Forest on limestone
Ironwood forest
Heath forest
Freshwater swamp forest

Subtropical and Temperate Upland
Forest (SUF)
Montane deciduous forest
Montane wet temperate forest
Subtropical broadleaf hill forest
Subtropical dry evergreen forest
Subtropical montane forest
Lower hill forest
Upper hill forest
Subalpine conifer forest
Subtropical pine forest

Alluvial Grassland / Subtropical Moist
Deciduous Forest (AGD)
Subtropical moist deciduous forests and
Grasslands in Ganges and Brahmaputra
River plains

Mangroves (MAN)
Mangrove
Freshwater Swamp forest associated
with mangroves

Degraded Forest (DEG)

Scrub (SCR)

Cleared/Agriculture

Unclassified

Perennial Lakes

International Boundaries

Railways

Perennial Rivers & Streams

Contour Lines
(3,000 Ft. Intervals)

Protected Area Boundaries

Names of protected areas are
provided only for those included
within TCUs. Areas for which
limits are not available are
indicated by circular boundaries
which reflect relative size.

Tiger Conservation Unit
Boundaries

Towns & Villages

28   Tiger Conservation Unit IDs

Sensitive Ecosystems Inventory — East Vancouver Island and Gulf Islands

British Columbia Conservation
Data Centre

*By Clover Point Cartographics
Ltd., Victoria, British Columbia,
Canada*

Contact:
Mike Shasko
cloverpoint@pinc.com

Software:
ARC/INFO Version 7.0.2
Hardware:
DEC Alpha
Plotter:
Hewlett–Packard DesignJet
2500
Data Source(s):
Baseline TRIM Mapping for
British Columbia and sensitive
ecosystem records

The Sensitive Ecosystems Inventory (SEI) series of 70 1:20,000-scale maps details fragile and/or rare vegetation along eastern Vancouver Island, British Columbia, Canada.

Vancouver Island's eastern coastal lowland and adjacent Gulf Islands comprise an ecological region unique in Canada. The Mediterranean-type climate and long growing season support many rare species of plants and animals as well as a variety of productive ecosystems. It is also one of two areas in British Columbia where the greatest loss of natural systems has occurred and continues to occur. Intense development pressures throughout this region have caused fragmentation and loss of most of these natural areas.

The SEI project identifies the remnants of these rare and fragile terrestrial ecosystems to encourage land-use decisions that will ensure their continued ecological integrity.

The SEI systemically identified, classified, mapped, and evaluated sensitive ecosystems throughout the coastal lowland. Approximately 9,000 sites were located in an area of roughly 5,000 square kilometers. The minimum mapping size for non-forested areas was one-half hectare. The minimum mapping size for forested areas varied based on age class and structural stage.

The initial phase of the SEI project involved the interpretation of approximately 3,000 aerial photos and the compilation of existing data. The second phase consisted of field checking approximately 26 percent of all sites identified in Phase 1 to verify boundaries, classify, photograph, and evaluate present conditions. The final phase involved compiling and editing all data, digitizing sites outlined on the air photos using the Mono Restitution method, and producing digital and hard-copy maps.

The SEI data is intended to be used for a variety of land-use planning processes.

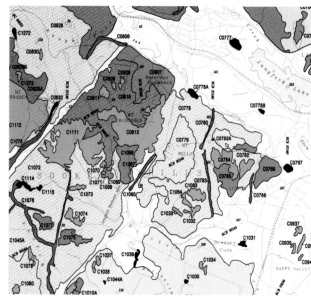

Terrestrial Ecoregions of Mexico

Conservation Science Program,
World Wildlife Fund,
Washington, D.C.

*By D. Olson, E. Dinerstein,
P. Hedao, S. Walters, C. Loucks,
and W. Wettengel*

Contact:
David Olson
david.olson@wwfus.org

Software:
ARC/INFO Version 7.1.2
Hardware:
Hewlett–Packard UNIX
workstations
Plotter:
Hewlett–Packard 650C and
755CM
Data Source(s):
CONABIO and published and
non-published sources

This map shows the ecoregions of Mexico. An ecoregion is a relatively large area of land or water that contains a geographically distinct set of natural communities that (1) share a majority of their species, ecological dynamics, and environmental conditions and (2) function together as a conservation unit at global and regional scales.

Mexican government and non-government conservation organizations can use this map in planning an ecoregion-based national conservation strategy. Ecoregion-based conservation (ERBC) is rapidly emerging as an approach the scale of which may best be suited for achieving the mission to save life on earth. Conservation strategies formulated at an ecoregional scale incorporate and are responsive to the spatial and temporal scales of the underlying ecological and evolutionary processes. The goals of biodiversity conservation are to

- Represent all distinct natural communities within conservation landscapes and provide a network of protected areas.
- Maintain ecological and evolutionary processes that create and sustain biodiversity.
- Maintain viable populations of species.
- Conserve blocks of natural habitat large enough to be resilient to large-scale periodic disturbances and long-term changes.

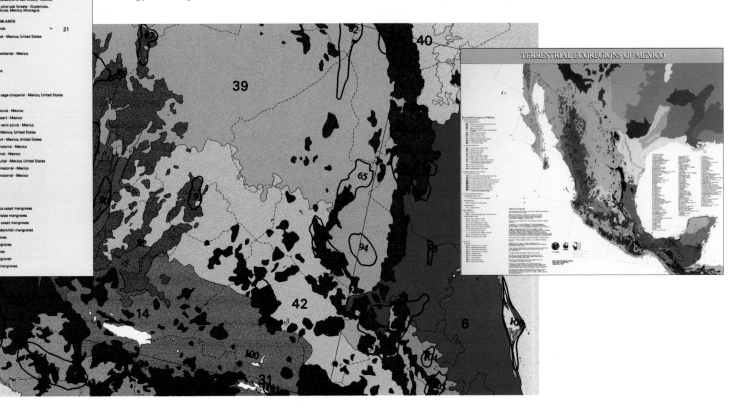

Philadelphia Crime Analysis and Mapping System (PhiCAMS)

Philadelphia Police Department,
Philadelphia, Pennsylvania

*By Robert Cheetham and
Kevin Switala*

Contact:
Robert Cheetham
cheetham@pobox.upenn.edu

Software:
ArcView GIS Version 3.1 and
ArcView Spatial Analyst
Hardware:
Windows NT 4.0 workstation on
Intel Pentium II
Plotter:
Hewlett–Packard 750C plus
Data Sources(s):
Incident Transmittal System and
QCVF vehicle recovery file

The Crime Analysis and Mapping Unit of the Philadelphia Police Department serves the needs of 7,000 police officers and 1,000 civilian personnel. Its integrated GIS enables the unit to plot maps with the latest and most accurate information. In addition to providing Intranet-based crime analysis tools to officers in the districts, the mapping unit produces maps of homicides, aggravated assaults, property crimes, vehicle-related crimes, rapes, robberies, and narcotics.

This map shows incidents categorized as gun crimes for the period January 1, 1998, through January 31, 1998. The second map indicates stolen vehicles from the 2nd District from March 1 through June 30, 1998, that were recovered by June 1998.

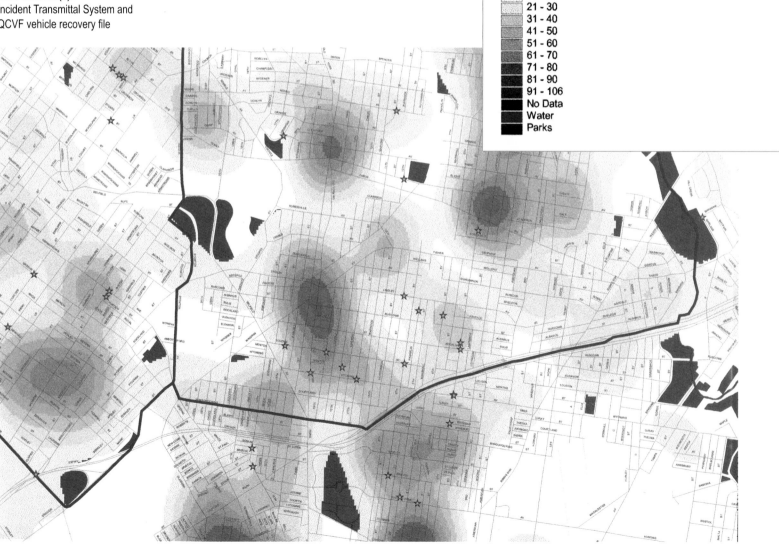

Firearms Violations
District Boundaries
Text Stname
Streets
Density from Gun Crimes (Agg Assault, Homicide, Robbery)
0 - 10
11 - 20
21 - 30
31 - 40
41 - 50
51 - 60
61 - 70
71 - 80
81 - 90
91 - 106
No Data
Water
Parks

June Recoveries

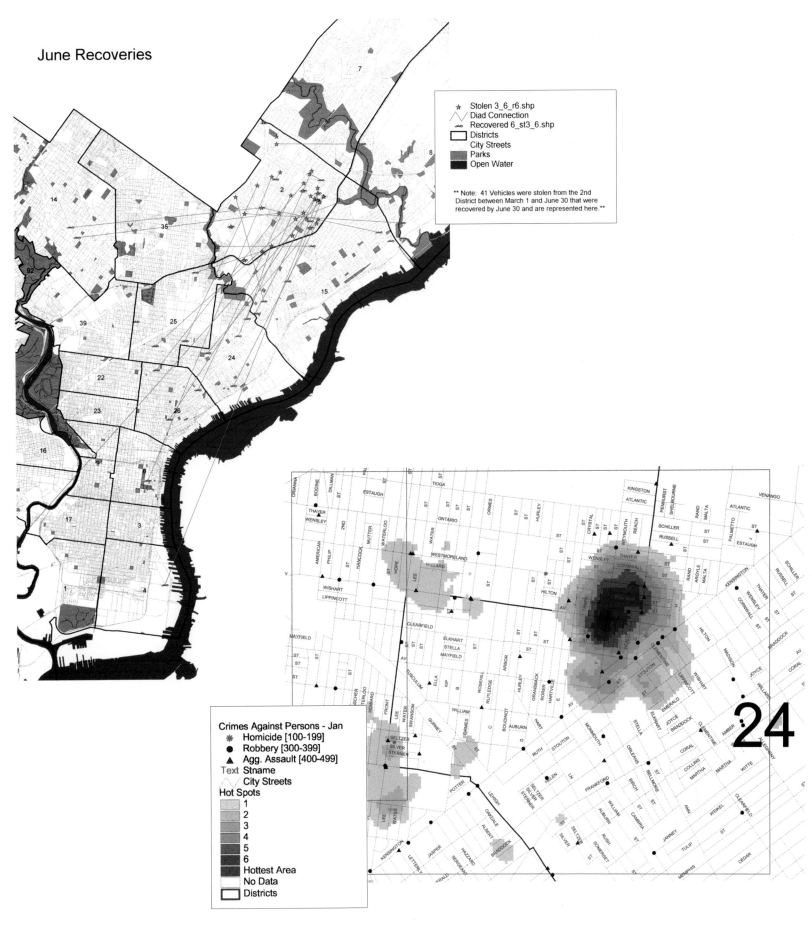

Stolen 3_6_r6.shp
Diad Connection
Recovered 6_st3_6.shp
Districts
City Streets
Parks
Open Water

** Note: 41 Vehicles were stolen from the 2nd
District between March 1 and June 30 that were
recovered by June 30 and are represented here.**

Crimes Against Persons - Jan
* Homicide [100-199]
● Robbery [300-399]
▲ Agg. Assault [400-499]
Text Stname
City Streets
Hot Spots
1
2
3
4
5
6
Hottest Area
No Data
Districts

24

San Diego Crime Maps

San Diego Police Department
(SDPD) Crime Analysis Unit,
San Diego, California

*By Chad Yoder and
Deena Bowman-Jamieson*

Contact:
Crime Analysis Unit
zgb@sdpd.sannet.gov

Software:
ARC/INFO Version 7.2.1 and
ArcView GIS Version 3.1
Hardware:
IBM RS/6000 AIX 4.2, Pentium II
Windows 98 workstation, and
Hewlett–Packard Vectra VL
Pentium II Windows 95
workstation
Plotter:
Hewlett–Packard DesignJet 3500
Data Source(s):
SDPD and SanGIS

City of San Diego, Gang Boundaries
This map depicts the distribution of gangs throughout the city of San Diego. Because of the challenge in representing overlap between gangs, SDPD chose to use the regions data model to create and maintain this information. The gang names were generalized for public display.

Scripps Mesa Service Area, Auto Theft and Recoveries of Toyotas and Hondas
Linkages between stolen and recovered Hondas and Toyotas for the Scripps Mesa Service Area are shown on this map. Interestingly, the average distance between the stolen and recovered vehicles is only 1.1 miles. This map demonstrates the need for a comprehensive analysis that includes tracking the time of day, day of week, and the condition of the recovered vehicle.

Citizen Narcotics Complaints and Narcotics Arrests, January–March 1999
This map shows the distance of narcotics arrests to citizen complaints using one-tenth-mile concentric buffers. Managers as well as crime analysts use this map to assess responsiveness to citizen complaints. Additionally, SDPD is relying on non-traditional police data, such as land use and orthophotos, to understand the conditions within the city.

Mid City Division Neighborhoods, Traffic Accident Density in Square Miles, July–December 1998
The density of serious injury, minor injury, non-injury, and no detail traffic accidents in the Mid City area are illustrated in this map. With the implementation of the photo, red-light project, a map such as this can be used by SDPD Traffic Division to identify intersections throughout the City of San Diego requiring photo, red-light cameras.

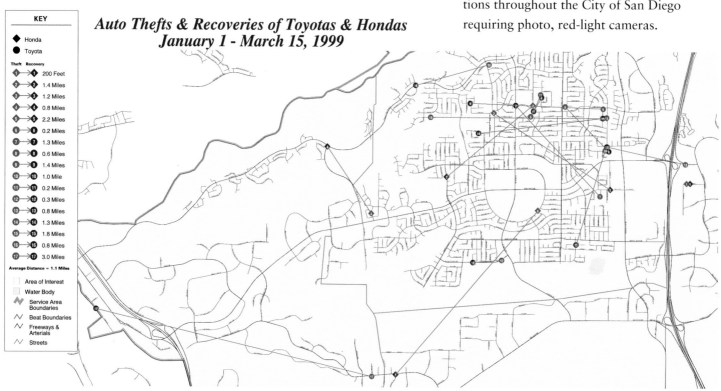

*Auto Thefts & Recoveries of Toyotas & Hondas
January 1 - March 15, 1999*

Citizen Narcotics Complaints & Narcotics Arrests
January - March, 1999

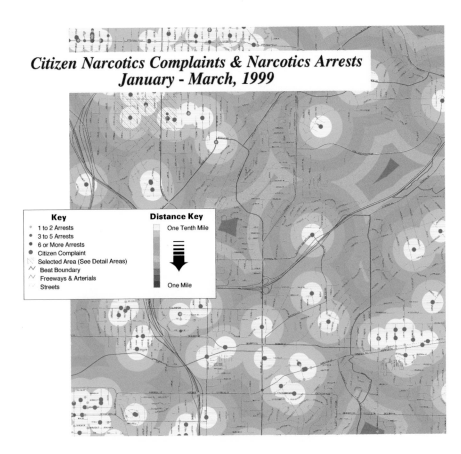

Key
- 1 to 2 Arrests
- 3 to 5 Arrests
- 6 or More Arrests
- Citizen Complaint
- Selected Area (See Detail Areas)
- Beat Boundary
- Freeways & Arterials
- Streets

Distance Key
One Tenth Mile

One Mile

Orthophoto of Selected Area

Land Use of Selected Area

- Single Family
- Multi-Family
- Commercial & Office
- Institutional
- Parks & Open Space
- Vacant

Gang Boundaries

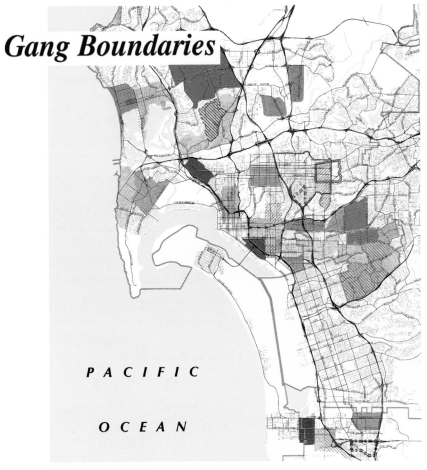

PACIFIC

OCEAN

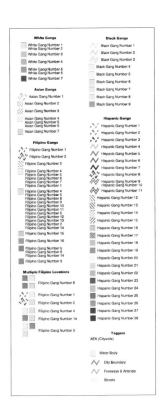

Landslide Hazard Susceptibility Maps for the San Francisco Bay Region: Tools for Emergency Planning During the 1997–98 El Niño

U.S. Geological Survey,
Menlo Park, California

By David Ramsey, Scott Graham, and the San Francisco Bay Landslide Team

Contact:
David Ramsey
dramsey@sierra.wr.usgs.gov

Software:
ARC/INFO Versions 7.0.4 and 7.1.1 and ARC GRID
Hardware:
Sun Ultra Enterprise 3000 running Solaris 2.5.1
Plotter:
Hewlett–Packard DesignJet 2500 CP
Data Source(s):
Open-file reports, USGS Professional papers, National Weather Service (NWS), and California Office of Emergency Services (OES) data

Landslides are an expensive, dangerous, and sometimes deadly geologic hazard in the San Francisco Bay region. They can damage or destroy homes, roadways, and utility infrastructure costing millions of dollars and endangering lives. Two types of slides are common in the San Francisco Bay region: (1) debris flows that occur in a single storm when prolonged, intense rain saturates the soil on steep slopes causing the soil to become unstable and move down slopes rapidly in a thin slurry and (2) slides and earth flows that are triggered by heavy rainfall over an entire season and deform the ground surface more slowly than debris flows.

Landslides occur during a normal San Francisco winter but can be especially numerous in an El Niño winter, which brings extra precipitation. In 1982, a particularly intense rainstorm triggered 18,000 debris flows causing $66 million in damage and 25 fatalities.

In anticipation of landslides associated with forecasts of heavy, El Niño precipitation in 1997–98, scientists and GIS specialists from the San Francisco Bay Landslide Team at the U.S. Geological Survey (USGS) created maps to assess the hazard in the San Francisco Bay region. These landslide susceptibility maps were generated at a regional and county scale and show areas where deadly debris flows were likely, as well as the amounts of rainfall needed to trigger them. Other maps outline areas of ancient landslides where slower moving, deep-seated slides and earth flows could occur.

As predicted, landslides were a prevalent geologic hazard during the 1997–98 El Niño winter along the California coast. In February, a series of El Niño-driven storms saturated the San Francisco Bay region triggering debris flows. As rainfall totals reached 200 percent of normal by midwinter, a number of slides and earth flows occurred.

In April and May 1998, the USGS conducted a field reconnaissance study in the San Francisco Bay area to provide a general overview of the landslide damage from the 1997–98 sequence of El Niño-related storms.

The study found that over 470 damaging landslides caused $140.93 million in damages and one fatality. Maps were generated showing the locations of the damaging landslides and provided details of the field reconnaissance. The data gathered from this study is being compiled in ARC/INFO as a spatial database and will be used for a variety of studies aimed at better understanding and predicting landslides in the San Francisco Bay area.

Topography plays a major role in the initiation of debris flows and the recognition of slides and earth flows. A shaded relief map was created from 35,000,000 digital elevations spaced 30 meters apart. The data set was assembled from 204 separate digital elevation models (DEMs) derived from topographic maps in the USGS 7.5' series. The DEMs were compiled into a single data set by the LATTICEMERGE command in ARC/INFO. Inconsistencies and edge-match problems between adjacent DEMs were resolved using the FOCALMEAN function in ARC GRID. Hill shading was prepared by the HILLSHADE command in ARC/INFO, using a sun azimuth of 315 degrees, a sun elevation angle of 45 degrees, and a vertical exaggeration of 2.0.

These maps are part of USGS Open-File Report 97-745, "San Francisco Bay Region, California, Landslide Folio." The complete report, including the ARC/INFO coverages and grids used to create the maps, is available online at http://wrgis.wr.usgs.gov/open-file/of97-745.

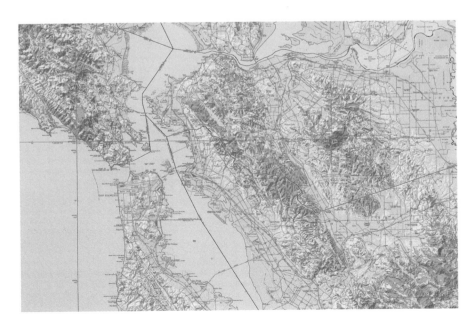

Storm Surge Predictions for Hurricane Landfalls in Glynn County, Georgia

Information Technology
Outreach Services, Georgia
Department of Transportation,
Georgia Emergency Manage-
ment Agency, Athens, Georgia

*By Eric James, Eric Sawyer, and
staff at I.T.O.S.*

Contact:
Eric Sawyer
info@itos.uga.edu

Software:
ARC/INFO and ArcView GIS
Hardware:
PC/Windows NT
Plotter:
Hewlett–Packard 755CM
Data Source(s):
Georgia State Clearinghouse,
National Weather Service
SLOSH model, and USGS digital
elevation model

This cartographic product uses Georgia's statewide GIS database as well as an evacuation route theme created from the State's Hurricane Evacuation Plan. The map was originally created as plot on four mounted panels. Georgia's hurricane planner uses this map in his office and during his travels to counties that face evacuation or host evacuees.

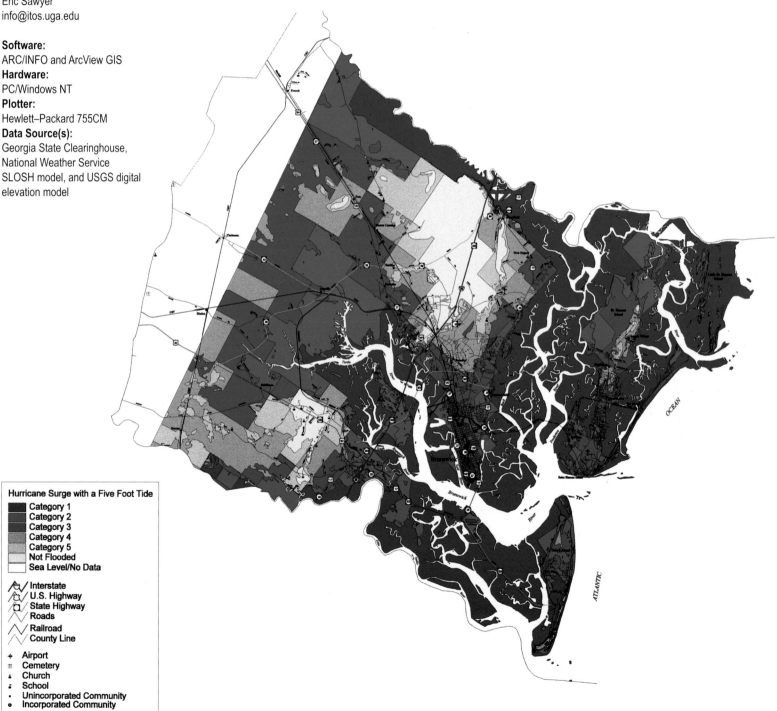

Hurricane Surge with a Five Foot Tide
- Category 1
- Category 2
- Category 3
- Category 4
- Category 5
- Not Flooded
- Sea Level/No Data

- Interstate
- U.S. Highway
- State Highway
- Roads
- Railroad
- County Line

- Airport
- Cemetery
- Church
- School
- Unincorporated Community
- Incorporated Community

MIKE21 (Danish Hydraulic Institute) 2-D Hydrologic Model

Mid-Pacific GIS, U.S. Bureau of
Reclamation, Sacramento,
California

*By M. Sebhat, T. Heinzer,
E. Robbins, D. Hansen, and
B. Simpson*

Contact:
M. Sebhat
msebhat@mp.usbr.gov

Software:
ARC/INFO Version 7.2.1,
ARCPLOT and ARC GRID
Hardware:
Hewlett–Packard UNIX server
and Windows NT workstation
Plotter:
Hewlett–Packard 2500CP
Data Sources(s):
USBR MPGIS hydrography and
transportation database, 10
meter SPOT imagery, and model
output from MIKE21

This map was prepared using ARC/INFO and ARCPLOT after modeling results from the MIKE21 model were translated back to ARC GRID format. Mid-Pacific GIS developed an ARC/INFO interface to DAMBRK in order to obtain the initial hydrograph and breach parameters for Monticello Dam. The hydrograph that resulted was used in MIKE21 to determine flood extent and depth.

The flood information in the Yolo Bypass was calibrated to the flood event of 1986 and was used as a hot-start scenario for the MIKE21 run. Levees were also used in the elevation lattice by inserting them using ARC GRID functions. The modeling environment did not erode levees but could overtop them. It was important to know the effect the levees would have in places such as Davis and Sacramento.

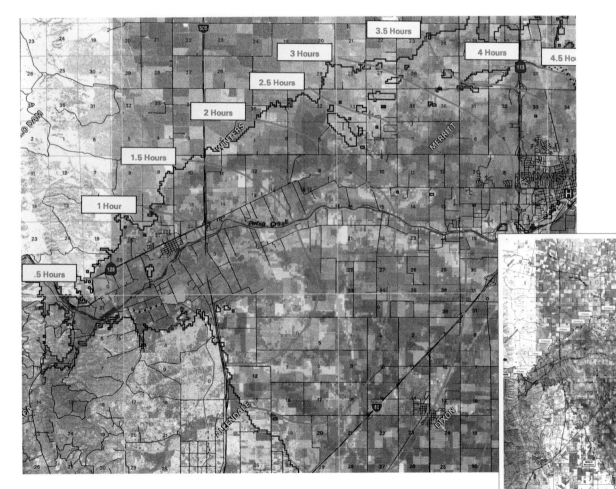

Number of Times the Land Has Burned

Geo-Cart Systems, Long Beach, California

By James Woods

Contact:
James Woods
jawoods-gcs@worldnet.att.net

Software:
Atlas GIS Version 2.1 (DOS) and Atlas GIS Version 4.0 (Windows)
Hardware:
Pentium PC
Plotter:
Output to eps file
Data Source(s):
Los Angeles County Department of Public Works and Los Angeles County Fire Department

This map represents the distribution of fire frequency in the Santa Monica Mountains and is part of an on-going study of the brush fire history of Los Angeles County. Originally, the study area only included the Santa Monica Mountains region, but it has expanded to include all of Los Angeles County. Other analyses and maps from this database were used by a local civil engineering firm in a study of post-fire debris production potential and by the Los Angeles County Fire Department to warn residents of potential brush fire hazard.

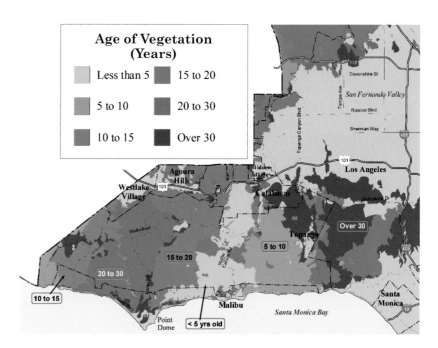

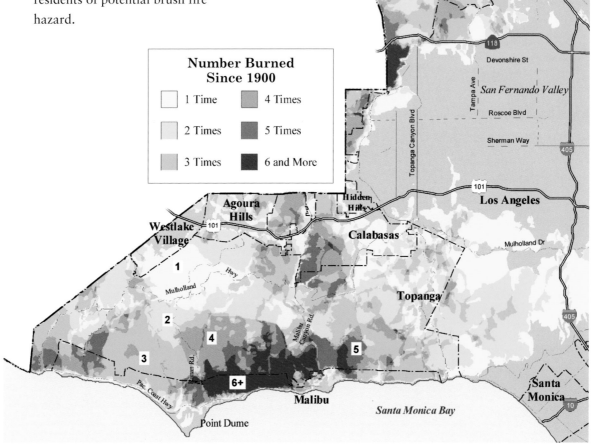

Piru Incident — Fire Perimeter and Ownership Map, Piru Watershed Damage
Juniper Incident — Operations Map

Ventura County Fire
Department, Camarillo,
California

*By Jim Kniss, Don Taylor, and
Rich Strazzo*

Contact:
Jim Kniss
jim.kniss@mail.co.ventura.ca.us

A final of the Piru Incident shows acreage of federally owned land burned. This wildfire burned over 12,500 acres in Ventura County, California, in October 1998. The map was created in two pieces to facilitate its incorporation into a final document.

The Watershed Damage Map for the Piru Incident was produced to assist the CDF rehabilitation team assess the damage to the Pole and Hopper Creek watersheds.

The Piru fire occurred at the same time as the Olgilvy fire. The Ventura County Fire Department's mapping section was instrumental in operating both GIS mapping sections at both fires.

The Operations Map for the Juniper Incident was used for briefing during the fire in September 1998. The Juniper fire damaged

Software:
ArcView GIS Version 3.1 and
ArcPress
Hardware:
Laptop computer
Plotter:
Hewlett–Packard 750C
Data Source(s):
Raster topography images, GPS
perimeter data, GPS structure
damage locations, and state
supplied watershed and
ownership boundaries

more than 30 structures in less than 48 hours. This map depicts the branches and divisions used for assignment of fire fighting teams. Also shown are locations of damaged structures and a digital photo of a burned-out area. The Ventura County application for displaying Incident Command System (ICS) symbology is highlighted here.

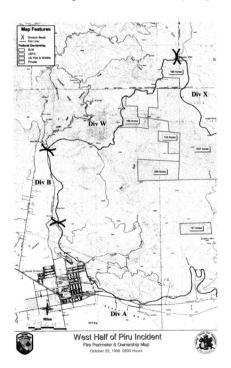

West Half of Piru Incident
Fire Perimeter & Ownership Map
October 22, 1998 0800 Hours

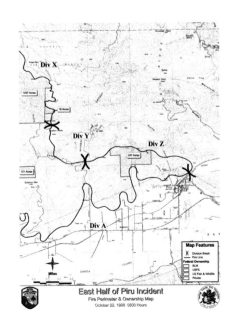

East Half of Piru Incident
Fire Perimeter & Ownership Map
October 22, 1998 0800 Hours

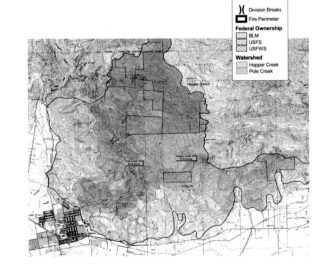

Using GIS for Utilities Management, Port of Beirut

Electric/Gas

Khatib & Alami (Consolidated Engineering Company), Beirut, Lebanon

By Nader Soubra

Contact:
Nader Soubra
nsoubra@gis.kacec.com.lb

Software:
ARC/INFO Version 7.2.1, ArcView GIS, and ArcCAD Version 13
Hardware:
Sun Ultra UNIX
Plotter:
Hewlett–Packard DesignJet 650C
Data Source(s):
AutoCAD utility drawings for the Port of Beirut

Facilities at the Port of Beirut were heavily damaged and needed extensive rehabilitation during the civil war. A ministerial committee was established in 1991 to oversee the rehabilitation and operation of the port facilities. In 1993, a new committee, headed by the Minister of Transit and Transportation, was assigned by the Council of Ministers to follow up on the implementation of the plans that were set in 1991. The rehabilitation of the port began with the development of a new master plan. This plan was developed with assistance from specialists from the Port of Marseilles of France.

The objective of the GIS project was to design a utilities maintenance application using ArcView GIS. The original data about the existing utilities, water, wastewater, electricity, and telephone lines was generated and saved in AutoCAD format. These AutoCAD files were converted to .DXF format and imported into the GIS environment using ArcCAD software.

After the data conversion and corrections were completed, a utilities maintenance application was developed using Avenue in ArcView GIS. The application incorporated the parameters used by port engineers to make decisions about maintaining, repairing, or replacing existing utilities. These tasks were accomplished by adding the existing utilities in GIS format, then entering the current status of each of them in the attribute tables. Finally, applications were developed to maintain these utilities.

Structural

Water

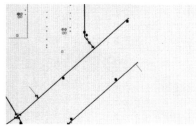

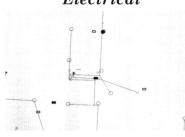

Electrical

Wastewater

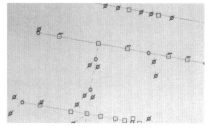

Port of Beirut
Beirut-Lebanon

Giselle Data Conversion Project Status Update

NESA, Sjaelland, Denmark

By Colleen A. Madigan

Contact:
Colleen A. Madigan
cmy@nesa.dk

Software:
ARC/INFO, ArcStorm, and
ArcView GIS Version 3.0a
Hardware:
IBM PC 300 GL
Plotter:
CalComp TechJet 5500
Data Source(s):
Kraks Geomarketing Package
and internal NESA utility data

NESA is Denmark's largest distributor of electricity. It serves the majority of Copenhagen's suburban municipalities in north Zealand and the municipalities in the area of Roskilde. The Giselle project, a spatial data conversion project, is 38 percent complete with 100 percent completion anticipated by 2000.

These maps were prepared to give NESA management and the GIS department a visual perspective of the spatial data conversion project. The maps also were prepared as internal and external marketing materials.

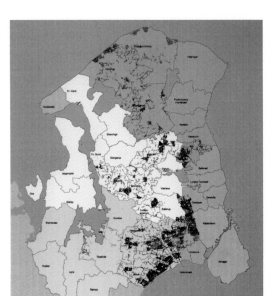

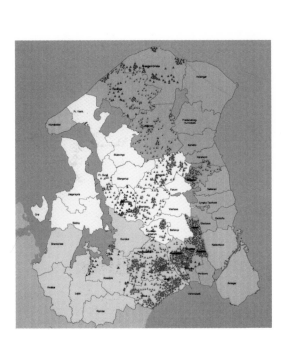

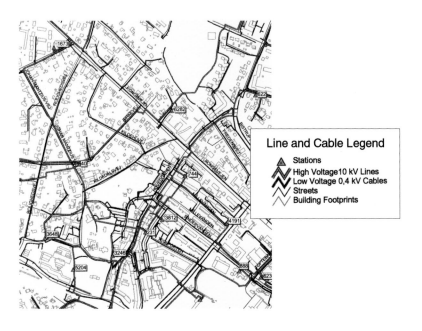

Line and Cable Legend

△ Stations
High Voltage 10 kV Lines
Low Voltage 0,4 kV Cables
Streets
Building Footprints

Washington Square in Holland, Michigan

Holland Board of Public Works,
Holland, Michigan

*By Brian Hayes and
Matt VanDyken*

Contact:
Brian Hayes
hayes@ci.holland.mi.us

Software:
ARC/INFO and ArcView GIS
Version 3.1
Hardware:
400 MHz PC Windows NT 4.0
Plotter:
Hewlett–Packard DesignJet
755CM
Data Source(s):
In-house

This is an actual work order print used for the reconstruction of a commercial district in Holland, Michigan. The work order is used to show the locations and correct connections of new underground electric facilities. All standard work orders are produced from an ARC/INFO-based editor/work order program that was developed in-house. Complex custom work orders are occasionally created in ArcView GIS.

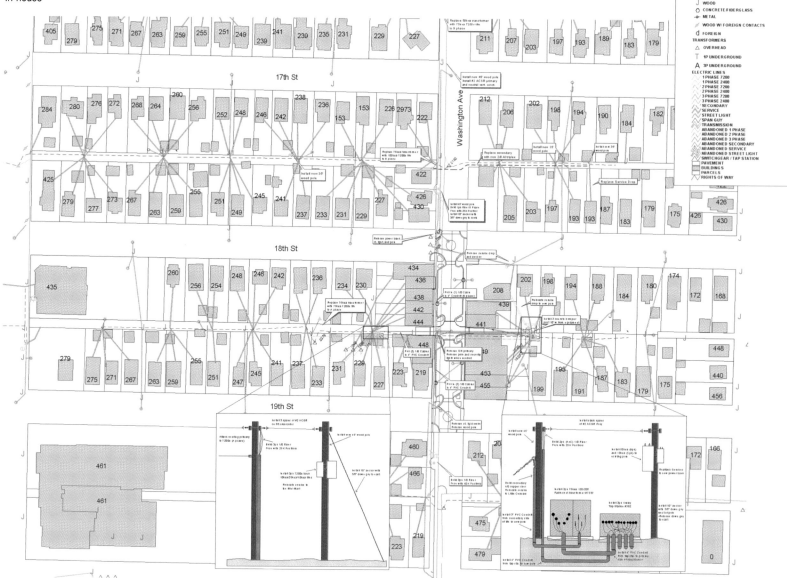

Vermont Bulk Power Electric Transmission System

Vermont Electric Power Company, Inc. (VELCO), Rutland, Vermont

By David B. Colman and Jarrod C. Harper

Contact:
Jarrod C. Harper
jharper@velco.com

The Vermont Electric Power Co., Inc. (VELCO), owns, operates, and maintains the high voltage transmission system in Vermont. It does not generate electricity, and its customers are the different utilities in the state.

This map shows the VELCO high voltage transmission system, interconnecting high voltage transmission systems, and the Vermont distribution utility sub-transmission systems. A double-sided, fortieth anniversary map, it was created in conjunction with an outside cartographer, Northern Cartographic.

The technical data on the transmission system was generated with ArcCAD. The data was exported to the cartographers who used ARC/INFO to complete the project. VELCO data was placed on top of their geographic data of Vermont. The final product was professionally printed.

Software:
ArcCAD and ARC/INFO
Hardware:
PC
Plotter:
Hewlett–Packard DesignJet 650C
Data Source(s):
Burlington Electric Department, Central Vermont Public Service Corporation, Inc., Citizens Utilities, Green Mountain Power Corporation, Hydro Quebec, Mass GIS – Executive Office of Environmental Affairs, Morrisville Water and Light Department, New England Power Pool, New England Power Service Company, Niagara Mohawk, Northern Cartographic, Public Service Company of New Hampshire, Vermont Center for Geographic Information, Village of Swanton Light and Water Department, and Washington Electric Co-op

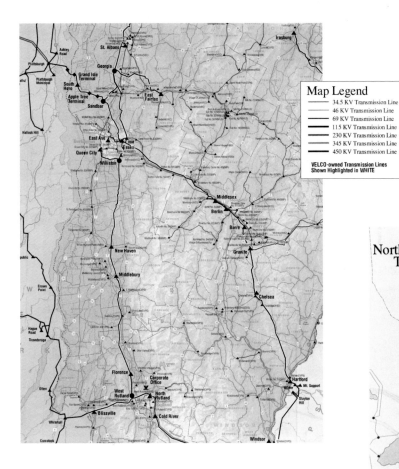

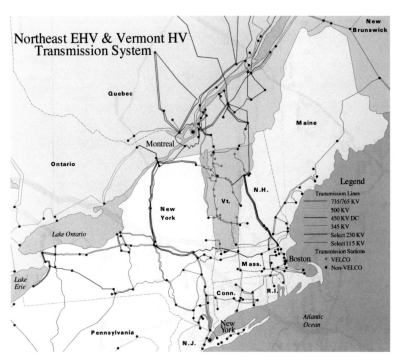

City of Winston–Salem Integrated Network Fire Operations (INFO) System and Fire Incident Analysis

City of Winston–Salem,
North Carolina

By Tim Lesser

Contact:
Tim Lesser
timl@ci.winston-salem.nc.us

Software:
ARC/INFO Version 7.2.1 and
ARC NETWORK
Hardware:
Sun Ultra 1 workstation
Plotter:
Hewlett–Packard 750C
DesignJet Color Plotter
Data Source(s):
City of Winston–Salem, North
Carolina and Forsyth County,
North Carolina

The City of Winston–Salem's Integrated Network Fire Operations (INFO) project, funded through a matching-funds Telecommunications and Information Infrastructure Assistance Program (TIIAP) grant from the U.S. Department of Commerce, facilitates communication among all fire stations and provides critical information in graphical form to the firefighters in emergency vehicles.

Integrated Services Digital Network (ISDN) technology provides the backbone for the network. The city has built a street centerline file using global positioning system (GPS) technology to provide the routing framework. GIS software uses the centerline network and alarm location to define an optimal route. Other graphical information is displayed such as the locations of hydrants, railroads, streams, and schools.

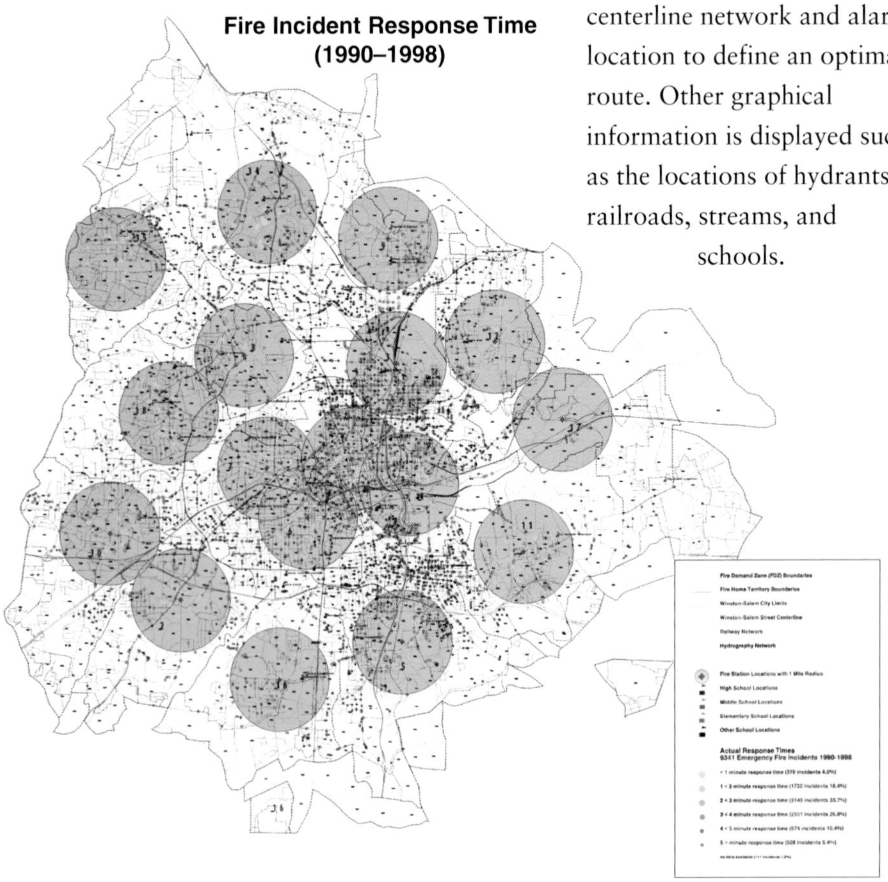

With the GIS, software firefighters are able to link, via icons and a touch-screen interface, to an imaging application. The application retrieves diagrams, floor plans, and document imaging details on pre-fire survey information, physically-challenged occupants, hazardous materials, and multiple address locations such as apartment complexes. This data at their fingertips improves firefighters' decision making during an emergency.

The fire incident analyses depicted on the following maps were derived using several data sets from the INFO project.

Fire Incident Response Time (1990–1998)
This map illustrates actual emergency-only fire incident response times for 1990–1998. One-mile fire station buffers are drawn to show the majority of the incidents were responded to in less than three minutes within this radius. As a whole, the majority of the fire incidents had response times of within four minutes.

Fire Station Response Allocations (1990–1998)
This map shows response allocation times for each fire station center via the street centerline derived from the ARC NETWORK module. Arc impedances, derived from segment length, mph, and lanes from the centerline attribute data, as well as turn-tables, are used for the calculation.

Emergency Fire Incidents (1990–1998)
This map spatially depicts emergency-only fire incidents for 1990–1998. One-mile fire station buffers are drawn to show the majority of the incidents occurred within this radius (approximately 65 percent).

Fire Incident Response Time (1990–1998)

FDZ Fire Incident Frequency (1990–1998)
This display is a thematic map of emergency fire incidents per fire demand zone (FDZ) for 1990–1998. The darker shade fills indicate an increase in the fire incidents within each FDZ during this period. Home territories are also drawn to show the frequency within this boundary.

Fire Incident First Response (1990–1998)
This map shows which fire stations first responded to a specific emergency fire incident for 1990–1998. The spider diagrams indicate which fire station (origins) responded to fire incidents (destinations) within their home territory and/or "cross" home territory boundaries.

Fire Incident First Response (1990–1998)

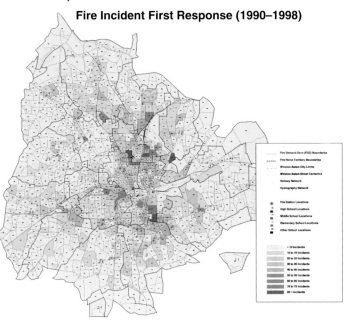

Fire Station Response Allocations (1990–1998)

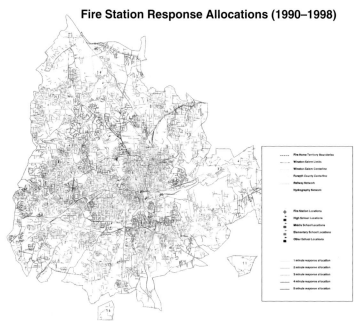

Emergency Fire Incidents (1990–1998)

FDZ Fire Incident Frequency (1990–1998)

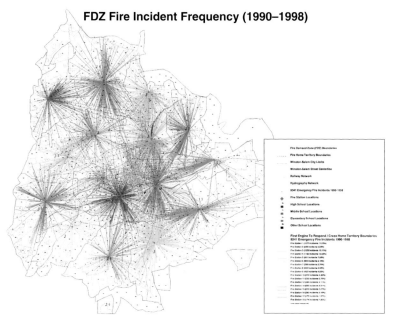

Multi-scale Map Series on Natural Resource Management in Ethiopia

Soil Conservation Research Programme, Ministry of Agruculture, Addis Abeba, Ethiopia, and Centre for Development and Environment, University of Berne, Berne, Switzerland

By Juerg Krauer, Andreas Heinimann, and Albrecht Ehrensperger

Contact:
Juerg Krauer
cde@giub.unibe.ch

Software:
ARC/INFO Versions 7.0.4 and 7.2.1
Hardware:
IBM RS/6000 and DELL Precision workstation 410
Plotter:
Hewlett–Packard DesignJet 650C
Data Source(s):
Landsat TM and Ethiopian Mapping Authority

Agriculture in Ethiopia is strongly influenced by socioeconomic and geo-ecological conditions. Food production is primarily subsistence-oriented and depends on climate, topography, and cultivation practices. Intensification of agricultural production to combat hunger and malnutrition requires decisive socio-political measures.

The Centre for Development and Environment (CDE) at the University of Berne, Switzerland, devised a long-term development program for the depleted Ethiopian highland, employing effective land-use concepts. This program is part of a comprehensive project that includes research and consulting by CDE in various African, Asian, and Latin American countries. The objective of the program is to increase land productivity in a sustainable manner by supporting efforts to enhance soil and water conservation in Ethiopia through research, human resource development, and institution building.

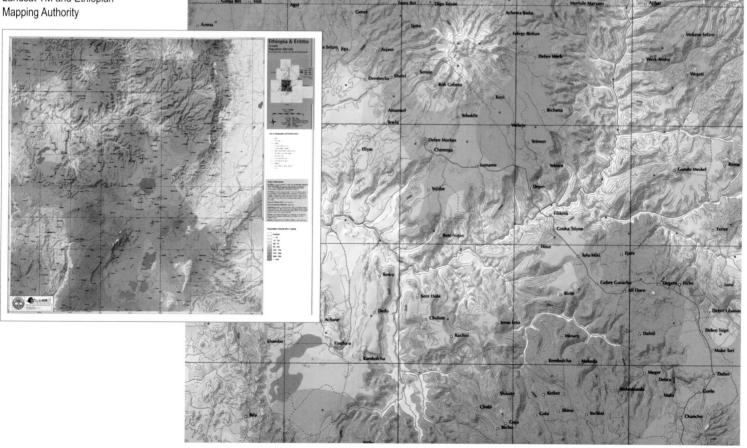

This map series details the various areas of
activity and the different scale levels of the
information system ETHIO-GIS of the Soil
Conservation Research Program (SCRP).
ETHIO-GIS is a spatial-temporal geographic
information system for natural resource
management and modeling.

GIS is used for developing numeric and
spatial models and for monitoring the project
areas. Politicians use GIS as a planning and
management tool, and agricultural consult-
ants use it as a methodological and educational tool.

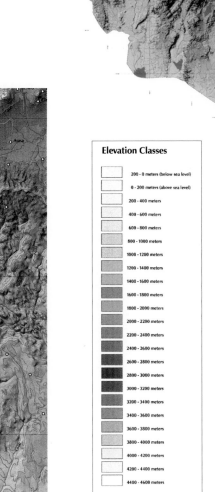

Elevation Classes

	200 - 0 meters (below sea level)
	0 - 200 meters (above sea level)
	200 - 400 meters
	400 - 600 meters
	600 - 800 meters
	800 - 1000 meters
	1000 - 1200 meters
	1200 - 1400 meters
	1400 - 1600 meters
	1600 - 1800 meters
	1800 - 2000 meters
	2000 - 2200 meters
	2200 - 2400 meters
	2400 - 2600 meters
	2600 - 2800 meters
	2800 - 3000 meters
	3000 - 3200 meters
	3200 - 3400 meters
	3400 - 3600 meters
	3600 - 3800 meters
	3800 - 4000 meters
	4000 - 4200 meters
	4200 - 4400 meters
	4400 - 4600 meters

Spatial and Temporal Variations in Particulate Matter Emission Rates from Agricultural Operations in the San Joaquin Valley of California

California Environmental
Protection Agency,
Air Resources Board,
Sacramento, California

*By Skip Campbell and
Dale Shimp*

Contact:
Skip Campbell
scampbel@arb.ca.gov

Software:
ARC/INFO Version 7.1.2
Hardware:
Microsoft Windows NT
workstation
Plotter:
Hewlett–Packard DesignJet
650C
Data Source(s):
California Department of Water
Resources, U.S. Department of
Agriculture, and Stephen P.
Teale Data Center

This map depicts the location and density of fine particulate matter (PM10) emission rates from agricultural land preparation and harvesting in California's San Joaquin Valley in the summer and fall. The PM10 emission rates were estimated using a method in the U.S. Environmental Protection Agency's Compilation of Air Pollution Emission Factors (AP-42) report.

This method uses area-specific farm activity and soil information to estimate PM10 emissions. The farm activity information was developed through a number of meetings with farmers and farm commodity experts from the San Joaquin Valley. These meetings identified the individual operations required to produce a crop of an individual farm commodity and the month of the year when the crop-specific field operation was most likely to occur.

Using the AP-42 equation, monthly emission densities were calculated by linking the month- and crop-specific activity data to a land-use data layer and incorporating a soil characteristics layer to identify the type of soil in which a particular crop was produced.

The land use data used to identify the location where specific crops were produced was obtained from the California Department of Water Resources. The soil classification data was based on soil data collected by the U.S. Department of Agriculture and modified by the California Air Resources Board for use in the AP-42 equations. Emission densities were mapped by overlaying the crop-specific land use coverage with the soil type coverage to identify the type of soil in which a particular crop was produced. This process links the soil information to the crop-specific activity information for a specific month, which allows the estimation of monthly PM10 emissions.

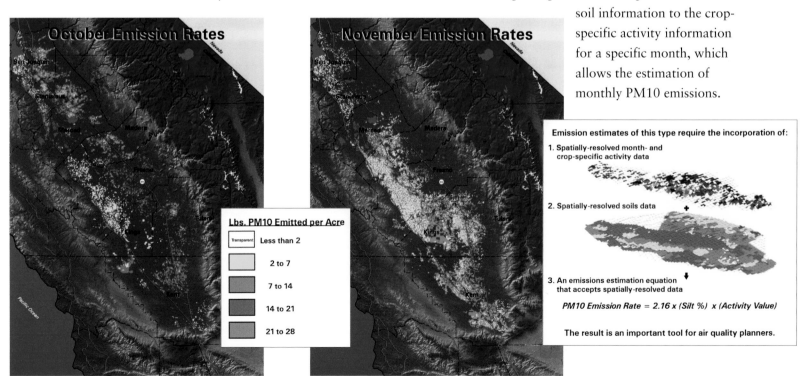

Emission estimates of this type require the incorporation of:

1. Spatially-resolved month- and crop-specific activity data

2. Spatially-resolved soils data

3. An emissions estimation equation that accepts spatially-resolved data

$$PM10\ Emission\ Rate = 2.16\ x\ (Silt\ \%)\ x\ (Activity\ Value)$$

The result is an important tool for air quality planners.

October Emission Rates

November Emission Rates

Lbs. PM10 Emitted per Acre

Transparent	Less than 2
	2 to 7
	7 to 14
	14 to 21
	21 to 28

Soil Survey and PRISM Map Automation Using ARCPLOT and AML

USDA–NRCS National Cartography and Geospatial Center, Forth Worth, Texas

By J. Steven Nechero and Robert Vreeland

Contact:
J. Steven Nechero
snechero@ftw.nrcs.usda.gov

Software:
ARC/INFO Version 7.1.1, ARCPLOT, AML, and ArcExplorer
Hardware:
Sun SPARCstation 20
Plotter:
ENCAD NovaJet
Data Source(s):
NOAA Cooperative station normals, NRCS SNOTEL station normals, Oregon State University, and supplemental data provided by regional and state climatologists and designated reviewers

The National Cartography and Geospatial Center (NCGC) developed a mapmaking system using ARCPLOT and AML to generate mean annual precipitation maps covering the period 1961–1990 for all 50 states. PRISM (Parameter-elevation Regressions on Independent Slopes Model) is an expert system that uses point data and a digital elevation model (DEM) to generate estimates of climate parameters.

Mean annual precipitation maps were developed by first using PRISM to calculate mean monthly precipitation layers and then summing these 12 layers. Each monthly precipitation layer was derived using all available and appropriate climate station data.

The mapping process has evolved from generating state and county map products to a regional approach. The regional coverage can be clipped into many different geographic entities. This approach is a multipurpose solution to serve cartographic production as well as data analysis in a GIS.

Much more information about technical aspects of PRISM, as well as downloadable PRISM data layers in a variety of formats can be obtained from the PRISM Web page at http://www.ocs.orst.edu/prism/prism_new.html.

NCGC is producing hard-copy maps and a CD–ROM set with ArcExplorer. PostScript files for the mean annual precipitation and ordering information for the CD–ROM set are at http://www.ftw.nrcs.usda.gov/prism/prism.html.

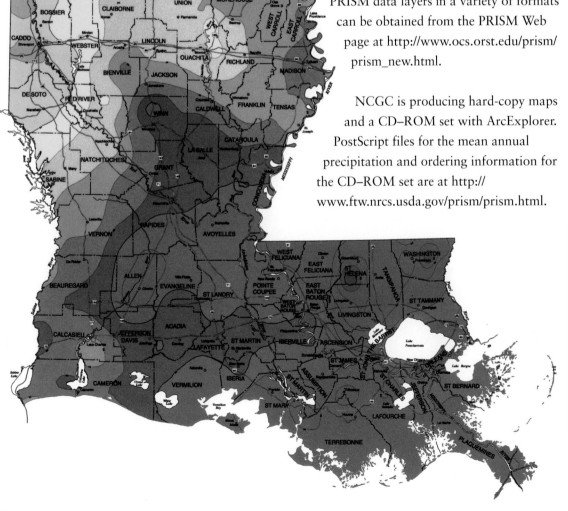

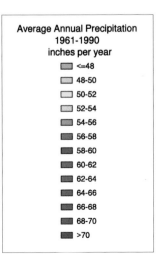

**Average Annual Precipitation
1961-1990
inches per year**

- <=48
- 48-50
- 50-52
- 52-54
- 54-56
- 56-58
- 58-60
- 60-62
- 62-64
- 64-66
- 66-68
- 68-70
- >70

Using ARC GRID to Inscribe Land Cover Patterns Derived from SPOT Imagery on Painted Relief

Bureau of Land Management,
Portland, Oregon

By Jeffery S. Nighbert

Contact:
Jeffery Nighbert
jnighber@or.blm.gov

Software:
ARC GRID, ARCPLOT, and
ArcPress
Hardware:
SGI Indigo II
Plotter:
NovaJet 50
Data Source(s):
10 Meter SPOT and 10 Meter
digital elevation models

This map illustrates a methodology and example, suitable for publication purposes, where SPOT imagery has been used to inscribe surface landscape patterns in a painted relief image. The result is a cartographic product that is more interesting and realistic, and maintains its integrity and standards of thematic mapping.

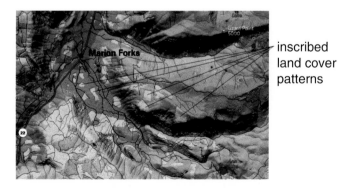

inscribed land cover patterns

Enlargment of the town, Marion Forks, and vicinity

1996 SPOT panchromatic image showing the same area

Farmland Preservation, Franklin County, Vermont

Cartographic Technologies Inc.,
Brattleboro, Vermont

*By David Greenewalt,
Susan Seymour, and Jon Caris*

Contact:
David Greenewalt
david@ctigis.com

Software:
ARC/INFO Version 7.1.1 and
ArcView GIS Version 3.0a
Hardware:
Pentium Pro 200
Plotter:
Epson 1520
Data Source(s):
Vermont digital orthophoto,
farmland coverage by CTI, and
roads and surface waters by
VCGI

The goal of the map series is to show the size and proximity of farms protected by the Vermont Housing and Conservation Board (VHCB) in Franklin and Addison counties of Vermont. This map and several others helped VHCB secure funding during the 1998 legislative session.

The aerial photography base allows the surrounding land use/land cover to be interpreted. A high level of detail can be displayed with fewer other data sets required (town lines, surface waters, and route numbers were added for reference). With its ability to apply a transparency effect on polygon fills, Corel Draw was used to highlight the protected farm properties without obscuring them.

1997 Common Snapping Turtle Telemetry Points

Department of Resources
Analysis, Saint Mary's University
of Minnesota, Winona,
Minnesota

By Jason Rohweder

Contact:
Jason Rohweder
jrohweder@emtc.er.usgs.gov

Software:
ArcView GIS Version 3.1 and
ArcView Spatial Analyst
Hardware:
Micron 300 PC
Plotter:
Hewlett–Packard DesignJet
2500CP
Data Source(s):
Upper Midwest Environmental
Sciences Center – Long Term
Resource Monitoring Program
(USGS), Inland Waterways Spill
Response Mapping Project
(EPA), and Wisconsin Depart-
ment of Natural Resources

This map was created to give the Wisconsin Department of Natural Resources a means to reference the distribution of the Common Snapping Turtle (Chelydra serpentina serpentina) telemetry points. The points were collected during the summer of 1997.

The background image was created using ArcView Spatial Analyst. The image is a composite of 1994 aerial photography and the Upper Midwest Environmental Sciences Center – Long Term Resource Monitoring Program. The location of the image is the middle section of Navigation Pool 8 of the Upper Mississippi River System just south of La Crosse, Wisconsin.

The telemetry points were used to help validate a Common Snapping Turtle habitat model as part of a master's thesis at Saint Mary's University of Minnesota.

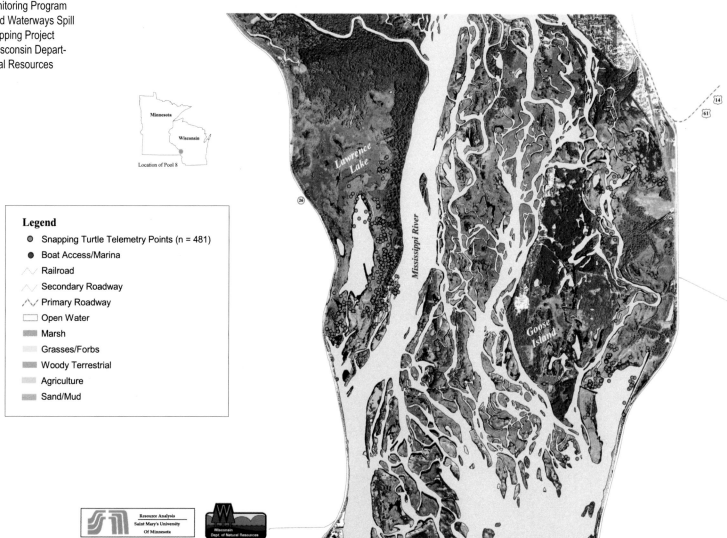

Legend

- ◎ Snapping Turtle Telemetry Points (n = 481)
- ● Boat Access/Marina
- ⋀⋁ Railroad
- ⋀⋁ Secondary Roadway
- ⋀⋁ Primary Roadway
- ▢ Open Water
- ▨ Marsh
- ▨ Grasses/Forbs
- ▨ Woody Terrestrial
- ▨ Agriculture
- ▨ Sand/Mud

Possible Environmental Impacts of the Breakdown of the Oil Products Pipeline in Section KRYRY-HAJEK

T-Mapy, Hradec Kralove, Czech Republic

By Miloslav Sindlar, Jan Kamenicky, and Lubomir Kriz

Contact:
Jan Kamenicky
tmapy@tmapy.cz

Software:
ARC/INFO Version 7.2.1 and ARC GRID
Hardware:
Sun UltraSPARC 5
Plotter:
Hewlett–Packard DesignJet 650C
Data Source(s):
Environmental institutions, private companies, and environmental studies

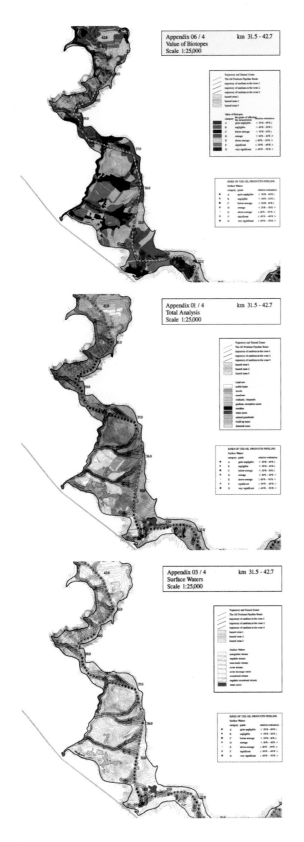

This map describes possible environmental impacts of the breakdown of the oil products pipeline in section KRYRY-HAJEK (pilot project).

Ecological and environmental specialists captured source data in the terrain. Captured information was drawn to maps, and the collected information was digitized from those maps. Digital data was analyzed with the analytical tools of ARC/INFO. The potential trajectories were produced with the ARC GRID module from a digital elevation model and resistance of environment data against medium movement (land use, streams). Important information was joined with pipeline trajectory at 100-meter intervals.

The final output is a result of multi-criteria analyses in LABE software. In the event of an accident, users can see the possible environmental risks at any point along the pipeline.

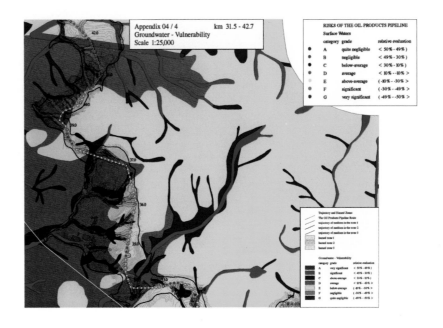

Alteration Zones, Mines and Prospects, and Dissolved Copper Concentration Water Quality Data Overlain on a Topographic Base for the Mt. Moly Region, Silverton, Colorado

U.S. Geological Survey,
Denver, Colorado

By Douglas B. Yager

Contact:
Douglas Yager
dyager@usgs.gov

Software:
ARC/INFO and ArcView GIS
Hardware:
UNIX server, PC
Plotter:
Hewlett–Packard DesignJet 650C
Data Source(s):
Winfield G. Wright, M. Alisa
Mast, Philip L. Verplanck, and
Christopher R. Ringrose

This map shows the combined impact that natural alteration and mining near the Mt. Moly region, Silverton, Colorado, have on waters draining this region. Less intensely altered zones are indicated in blue and green. Zones of more intense alteration are displayed in yellow, orange, and red. Dissolved copper abundances in waters are indicated, which exceed the current Colorado Basic Stream standards. Recommended copper abundances are exceeded in naturally altered but unmined and in mined locations.

Water quality data sampled downstream from natural and mining-related sources as part of the U.S. Geological Survey, Bureau of Land Management, U.S. Forest Service, and Environmental Protection Agency, Abandoned Mine Lands (AML) project indicates that AML restoration is not simply a mine waste-pile cleanup issue. Natural sources of chemical loading must be accounted for in altered regions before establishing achievable restoration goals.

Geologic, hydrologic, mining, and topographic data integrated into a GIS greatly assists in distinguishing between waters that are impacted by naturally altered by unmined and mined areas. A GIS approach to interpreting this data helps to determine how and where waters are adversely impacted and provides a visually intuitive approach to investigate natural geochemical background and mining-related environmental issues.

Stream sampled below known mining activity

Spring sampled above any known mining activity

⚒	Past producing mine location
●	Water sample site where dissolved metal concentrations exceed the State of Colorado Water Quality standards

Mapping the Geology of Illinois, Villa Grove Quadrangle, General Aquifer Sensitivity Map

Illinois State Geological Survey, Champaign, Illinois

By B. Stiff, R. Krumm, C. Abert, S. Beaverson, C. Goldsmith, C. McGarry, R. Nagy, D. Nelson, M. Riggs, and L. Smith

Contact:
C. Abert
abert@isgs.uiuc.edu

Software:
ARC/INFO Version 7.2.1
Hardware:
Sun SPARCstation 5
Plotter:
Hewlett–Packard 750C
Data Source(s):
ISGS

The potential for contaminating aquifers is a critical concern in Illinois and on the Villa Grove Quadrangle because chemical or biological agents from waste introduced into aquifers present potential health hazards. Residents on the Villa Grove Quadrangle rely totally on groundwater for their drinking water.

Aquifers are earth materials that yield groundwater to wells and are sensitive to contamination because their properties enable waste effluents to travel rapidly. They are composed of porous, coarse-grained sand and gravel deposits in glacial drift, and porous or fractured bedrock. Silty and clayey river and lake sediment in valleys and low-lying areas and diamicton on uplands are all fine-grained materials and not considered aquifers.

This aquifer sensitivity analysis rates geologic materials to a depth of 100 feet according to their capacity to protect the uppermost aquifer from potential contamination from a variety of sources.

Soil Pesticide Leaching Classes

High
Moderate
Somewhat Limited
Limited
Very Limited
Unknown
Water

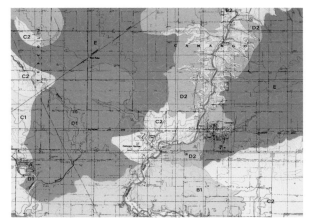

Soil Nitrate Leaching Classes

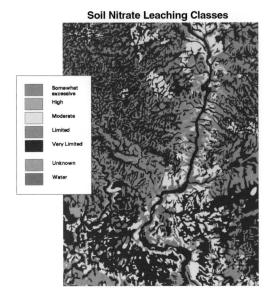

Somewhat excessive
High
Moderate
Limited
Very Limited
Unknown
Water

Aquifer Sensitivity to Nitrate Leaching

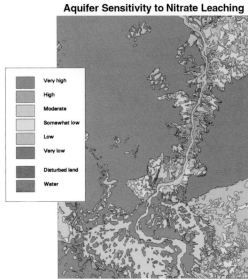

Very high
High
Moderate
Somewhat low
Low
Very low
Disturbed land
Water

Aquifer Sensitivity to Pesticide Leaching

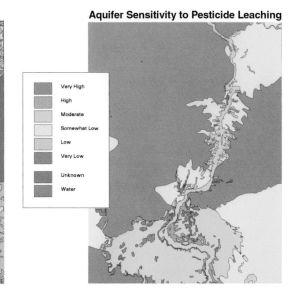

Very High
High
Moderate
Somewhat Low
Low
Very Low
Unknown
Water

The Maine Oil Spill Information System (MOSIS) — Environmental Vulnerability Index (EVI)

Maine Department of
Environmental Protection,
Augusta, Maine

*By Christopher Neal Kroot,
David Pollock, James Richards,
and Khaled Hassen*

Contact:
Christopher Kroot
christopher.kroot@state.me.us

Software:
ARC/INFO and ArcView GIS
Hardware:
UNIX Sun Solaris
Plotter:
Hewlett–Packard 2500
Data Source(s):
Maine Geologic Survey, Maine
Office of GIS, Maine Department
of Marine Resources, Maine
Department of Inland Fisheries
and Wildlife, and U.S. Fish and
Wildlife Service

The EVI Atlas is used to assist in emergency oil spill contingency planning, response, cleanup, and shoreline assessment. A primary objective has been to have an atlas that would be used by all the major cooperators in emergency oil spill response.

Currently, the Maine Department of Environmental Protection, Maine Department of Marine Resources, Maine Department of Inland Fisheries and Wildlife, the U.S. Coast Guard, NOAA, private cleanup companies, and the oil industry all use the EVI Atlas. The EVI helps to determine how to maximize the effective deployment of response resources in the event of an oil spill.

The data on the atlas maps is categorized by coastal marine geologic environments, land and water, roads and boundaries, marine resources and habitats, and coastal wildlife resources.

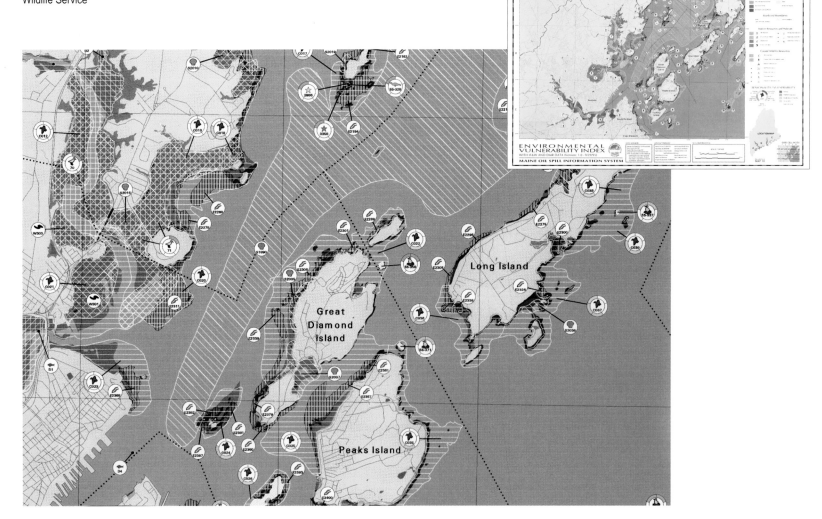

Informational Analytical System on Prevention of Dangerous Environmental Situations in Kiev

ECOMEDSERVICE,
Kiev, Ukraine

By S.V. Zorin, O.N. Kartavtsev, and A.D. Senchenko

Contact:
S.V. Zorin
ems@zorin.kiev.ua

Software:
ArcView GIS

Kiev, the capital of Ukraine, with more than two million people, is home to one fifth of the Ukraine population. Industrial emissions from stationary sources adversely affect the city's air quality. Since 1996, the Informational Analytical System has been addressing the prevention of dangerous environmental situations in the Kiev City "ecoGIS-KIEV." The Register of Stationary Emission Sources (RSES) was developed and over the next five years, RSES will monitor environmental risks and emission sources. The system, with its network of workstations, enables environmental protection specialists to compile information about environmental risks, emission source characteristics, and emission source composition in one database.

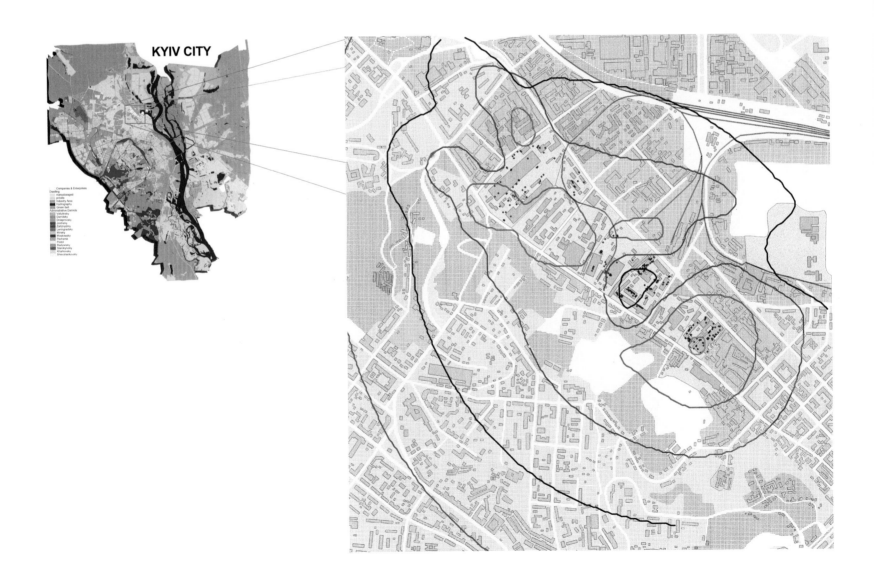

Shaded Relief Map of the Canadian Cordillera and Adjacent Regions

Geology

Geological Survey of Canada

*By Robert B. Kung and
Brian Sawyer*

Contact:
Robert Kung
kung@pgc.nrcan.gc.ca

Software:
ARC/INFO Version 7.0.4
Hardware:
Sun SPARCstation 20
Plotter:
Hewlett–Packard DesignJet 650C
Data Source(s):
Geological Survey of Canada,
Geomatics, Canada, USGS
EROS Data Center, and NOAA

This shaded relief map of the Canadian Cordillera was a by-product of the Geological Survey of Canada (GSC) Neotectonic Assemblage Map project. In modified form, it provides the backdrop for neotectonic data compiled by the GSC. The map was created as a tool for geologists identifying morphological areas of interest, while at the same time, it is an aesthetically pleasing cartographic product.

Cartographic balance and simplicity were objectives, and the eye is drawn to the oblique linearity and dramatic morphology of the Cordillera, which has been enhanced with hill shading and a realistic color palette. The cultural features on the map give the viewer a sense of location in the real world.

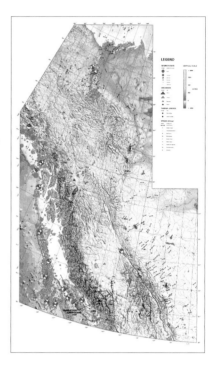

The topographic/ bathymetric data for the map was compiled mainly from GSC data, with supplementary data for adjacent regions coming from Geomatics Canada and the USGS EROS Data Center. GSC topographic data was derived by digitizing previously published analog topographic maps at one-kilometer grid intervals. A TIN was created using more than five million data points generated from ASCII text files. The TIN was then interpolated into a grid at 500-meter intervals using bilinear interpolation. The creation of a TIN this large was computationally intensive and required massive amounts of temporary storage. A TIN was created to ensure the greatest possible accuracy.

The interpolated lattice was then merged with other data sets, using the GRID MERGE function. Filtering and FOCALMEAN were used to smooth out data set boundaries. The completed lattice was processed as an HSV grid composite for the final map. Slicing the lattice using re-map tables created by the GRID command, CREATEREMAP, and then using the SLICE

function to create the derivative grids generated the hue and saturation components. The hue for the map's bathymetry is the same blue shading, with decreasing depth effect achieved by decreasing the saturation to zero as the water depth approaches zero. The topography of the map uses hues ranging from green at sea level to yellow, orange, and finally red at the highest elevations. Saturation of the topography also decreases to zero with the increase in elevation, which results in a color scheme the eye can accept as quasi-realistic.

The value component of the composite is the most important aspect of the map because it gives the map its hill shading and brings out the underlying landforms. Selection of sun azimuth and angle is important to the final appearance of the map. Although shading from the northwest is traditional in cartography, a sun azimuth from the northeast was chosen. Northeast shading serves to highlight the northwest–southeast trending linearity of the Cordillera, which is the result of offshore-displaced accreted terrains.

Blocky shorelines resulting from the lattice were matched to the actual shoreline by buffering a shoreline coverage appropriate for the map scale and using the resulting polygons to reset the hue and saturation to its appropriate cell values. This depended on whether the cell was in a land polygon or a water polygon.

A second edition of this map is planned, which will be significantly different in layout and presentation. New surface scene functionality available with ARC/INFO Version 7.2 will

facilitate the creation of more effective and interesting inset maps. New data will be incorporated, with greatly improved bathymetry in the Arctic Ocean and the Gulf of Alaska. New topography will include a large portion of Alaska and the extension of the Northwest Territories to include Victoria Island.

Copies of the map (Open File No. 3575) are $25 (Canadian), and are available from the GSC Map and Publication Sales Office at 101-605 Robson Street, Vancouver, BC, Canada V6B 5J3; 604.666.0271; 604.666.1337 (fax).

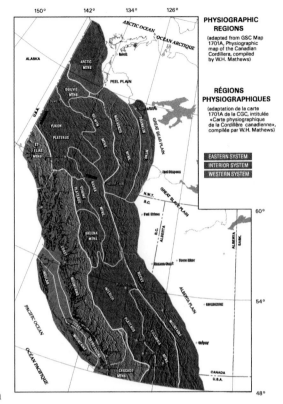

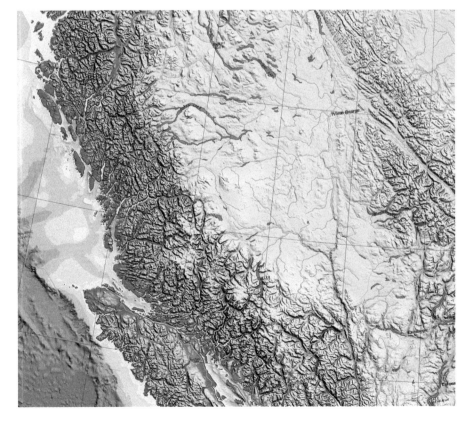

Seismic Building-Design Maps for the International Building Code

U.S. Geological Survey, Denver,
Colorado

*By Ken Rukstales,
E.V. Leyendecker, and
Arthur Frankel*

Contact:
Ken Rukstales
rukstales@usgs.gov

Software:
ARC/INFO and AML
Hardware:
UNIX workstation
Plotter:
Hewlett–Packard DesignJet 650C
Data Source(s):
USGS

U.S. Geological Survey (USGS) probabilistic seismic hazard maps for the United States are the basis for seismic building design maps developed for the National Earthquake Hazards Reduction Program and the year 2000 International Building Code. The design maps are a combination of the USGS probabilistic seismic hazard maps and deterministic hazard maps based on known seismic parameters of selected active faults. A set of rules was developed to merge the two distinct hazard maps and arrive at the seismic building design maps.

The probabilistic hazard maps and the deterministic hazard maps were produced using ARC/INFO. An AML procedure was written to apply the given rules to merge the two data sets on a polygon-by-polygon basis.

National maps of earthquake shaking hazards provide information essential to creating and updating the seismic design provisions of building codes used in the United States. Buildings, bridges, highways, and utilities built to meet modern seismic design provisions are better able to withstand earthquakes, not only saving lives but also enabling critical activities to continue with less disruption immediately after an earthquake.

America's first line of defense against earthquakes historically has been the construction of buildings that can withstand severe shaking.

More than 20,000 cities, counties, and local government agencies use building codes to help establish the construction requirements necessary to preserve public health and safety in earthquakes.

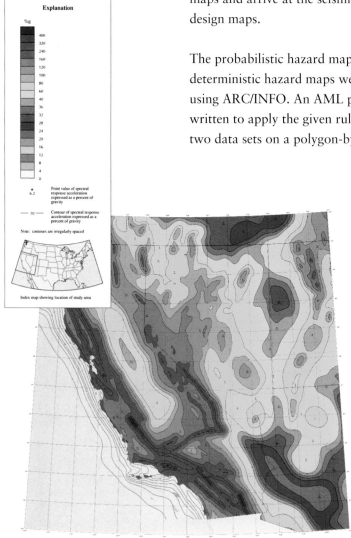

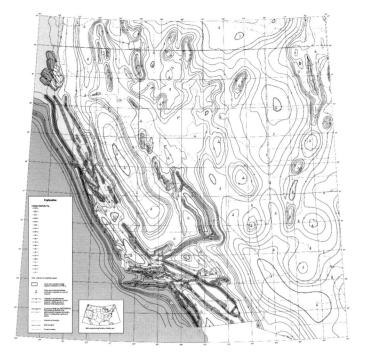

Digital Paleo-elevation Modeling for Reconstruction of Late Wisconsinan and Holocene Paleo-geography of the Great Lakes Region

Geological Survey of Canada (Atlantic), Bedford Institute of Oceanography, Dartmouth, Nova Scotia, Canada

By P.L. Gareau, C.F.M. Lewis, A.G. Sherin, and R. Macnab

Contact:
P.L. Gareau
pgareau@nrcan.gc.ca

Software:
ARC/INFO Version.7.0.4, ARCEDIT, ARCPLOT, and ARC GRID
Hardware:
Hewlett–Packard 9000 Series 700 workstation
Plotter:
ENCAD NovaJet 50
Data Source(s):
Canadian Hydrographic Service and National Geophysical Center of NOAA

The Great Lakes basins were loaded and isostatically depressed by the Laurentide Ice Sheet during the last glacial maximum about 21,000 to 18,000 years ago on the radiocarbon timescale (21–18ka BP). After about 14ka, a series of pro-glacial lakes formed shorelines in the ice-marginal depression as the ice edge melted and retreated toward its thickest zone around Hudson Bay. These once-level water planes were differentially uplifted in a northerly direction. The rate of uplift was rapid at first but declined exponentially with time and continues today as evidenced by historical water-level monitoring in the present lakes.

Recent geodynamic modeling of this process has been quite successful in using the global pattern of relative sea level change and regional geomorphic evidence of ice retreat to estimate the histories of ice loading and unloading, and vertical deflection of the earth's crust.

Regional application of these models has shown that they broadly track the known geological history of the Great Lakes, but they are not yet fine-tuned to closely simulate geological observations of former lakes in the Great Lakes basins. The map shows postulated shorelines for the Great Lakes at 5,000 and 10,000 Cal years BP.

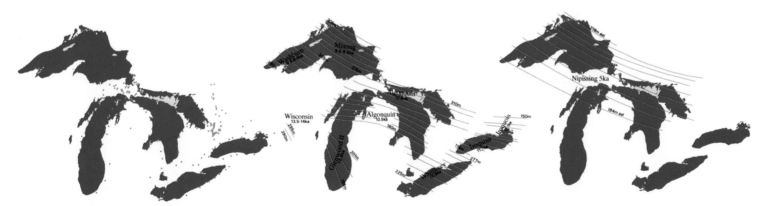

10Ka TOPOGRAPHY

5Ka TOPOGRAPHY

GeoMap Vancouver: Geological Map of the Vancouver Metropolitan Area

Geological Survey of Canada,
Pacific Division, Vancouver,
British Columbia, Canada

*By Robert J. W. Turner,
John J. Clague, Bertrand J.
Grouix, Robert Cocking, Andrew
Makepeace, Kazuharu
Shimamura, and Sonia Talwar*

Contact:
Robert Cocking
rcocking@gsc.nrcan.gc.ca

Software:
ARC/INFO Version 7.1.1
Hardware:
Sun SPARCstation 20, DEC
Alpha 3000, Intel PCs
Plotter:
Printed
Data Source(s):
Government of British Columbia,
TRIM data, NTDB data from
Geomatics, Canada, and
proprietary sources

GeoMap Vancouver displays the physical setting of the Greater Vancouver region. Cross-sections show the formation of the earth beneath the city, and inset maps portray various geological issues such as risks from earthquake liquefaction, floods, landslides, and the location of groundwater sources.

The main map focuses on the detailed surface distribution and bedrock geology of the region. The lack of geological jargon makes this product a valuable educational tool for students and non-geologists.

Beneath Vancouver

This three-dimensional perspective view illustrates the subsurface geology of Vancouver and the Fraser Valley. Knowledge of geology at depth comes from drill holes and geophysical surveys.

Physiography

Physiography is the surface form of the earth. The Vancouver region includes three main physiographic areas. Mountain areas comprise rugged bedrock ridges, peaks, and intervening steep-walled valleys. The larger valleys contain thick modern and Ice Age sediments and host large lakes and streams. The other two physiographic areas are within the Fraser Valley. Higher parts of the Fraser Valley are gently rolling uplands, ranging from about 15 meters to 250 meters above sea level. Thick Ice Age sediments, largely of glacial origin, underlie uplands. Flat lowlands occur along the Fraser River and its tributaries and are underlain by modern sediments.

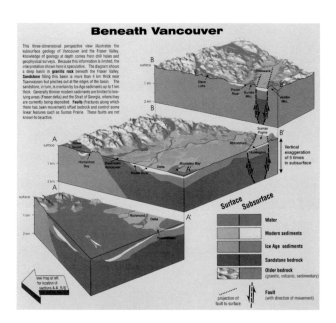

Physiography of GeoMap

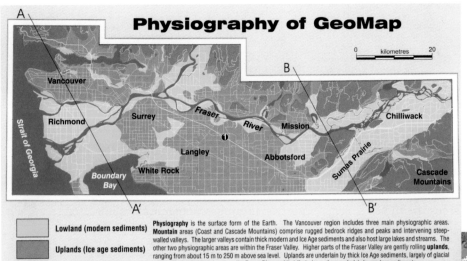

Physiography is the surface form of the Earth. The Vancouver region includes three main physiographic areas. **Mountain** areas (Coast and Cascade Mountains) comprise rugged bedrock ridges and peaks and intervening steep-walled valleys. The larger valleys contain thick modern and Ice Age sediments and also host large lakes and streams. The other two physiographic areas are within the Fraser Valley. Higher parts of the Fraser Valley are gently rolling **uplands**, ranging from about 15 m to 250 m above sea level. Uplands are underlain by thick Ice Age sediments, largely of glacial origin. Flat **lowlands** occur along the Fraser River and its tributaries and are underlain by modern sediments.

Legend:
- Lowland (modern sediments)
- Uplands (Ice age sediments)
- Mountains (bedrock)

Earthquake Ground Motion

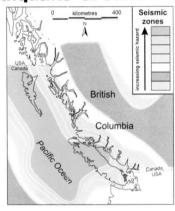

Seismic zones — increasing seismic hazard

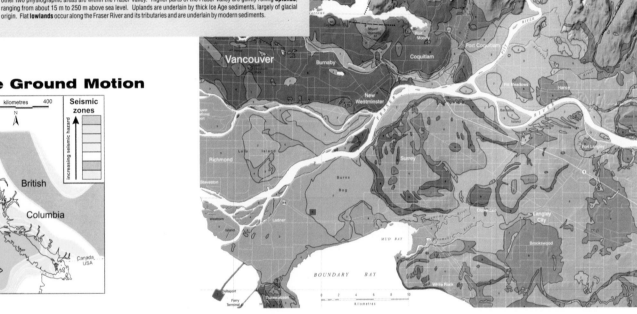

Groundwater and Aquifers

Aquifers are bodies of sediment or rock that are saturated and sufficiently permeable to provide subsurface water to wells. Most groundwater in the Fraser Valley is derived from aquifers in modern and Ice Age sediments. These aquifers are a major source of high-quality water for drinking and other uses. The British Columbia Ministry of Environment, Lands and Parks has classified 71 aquifers in the Fraser Valley according to current levels of use and vulnerability to contamination. Almost two-thirds of the aquifers are shallow and can be easily contaminated by downward infiltration of waters laced with agricultural fertilizers and pesticides, manure, septic effluent, or gas and oil from leaking storage tanks. The most heavily utilized of these highly vulnerable aquifers occur in the Abbotsford and Langley/Brookswood areas. Less developed, but highly vulnerable aquifers

occur in sediments below the floodplain and delta of the Fraser River. Deeper aquifers overlain by silts, clays, or tills of low permeability are less vulnerable to contamination. The most important of these deep aquifers occur in the Aldergrove area; others underlie the uplands of Vancouver, Burnaby, Surrey, and Langley, and the lowland of the Nicomeki and Serpentine rivers. Some groundwater is also pumped from fractured bedrock, for example, at Grant Hill, Mission, and Belcarra. The thin soil cover over these bedrock aquifers makes them highly vulnerable to contamination. Some aquifers, in both sediments and bedrock, have poor water quality due to elevated levels of naturally occurring substances such as chloride, iron, sulphur, and fluoride.

Legend:
- Aquifers not assessed
- Aquifers in Bedrock — high vulnerability
- Aquifers in Sediment:
  - high vulnerability heavy use
  - moderate to high vulnerability low to moderate use
  - low vulnerability low to heavy use

Brookswood aquifer · Abbotsford aquifer

Slopes and Landslides

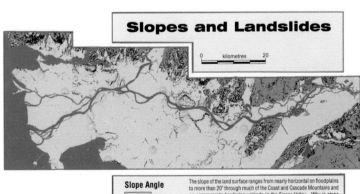

Slope Angle
- < 10°
- 10 - 20°
- > 20°
- landslide

The slope of the land surface ranges from nearly horizontal on floodplains to more than 20° through much of the Coast and Cascade Mountains and on escarpments bordering uplands in the Fraser Valley. Why is slope important? First, it affects surface drainage -- in a general sense, drainage improves as the land surface steepens. Second, slope is an important factor in the stability of the land surface -- most landslides in the Vancouver area occur on slopes that are steeper than 20° (red areas on this map). Locations of many of the landslides that have occurred in this century in the Fraser Valley are plotted on the map (landslides in the Coast and Cascade Mountains are not included). Most landslides in the Fraser Valley involve Ice Age sediments and are triggered by intense rainstorms. In contrast, many of the landslides in the Coast and Cascade Mountains are in bedrock (**rockfalls** and **rockslides**). A common type of landslide in both regions is rapid flows of water-saturated debris (**debris flows**).

Locations of landslides from Armstrong and Hicock 1979, 1980 (see ADDITIONAL INFORMATION) and G.H. Eisbacher and J.J. Clague, 1981, Urban landslides in the vicinity of Vancouver, British Columbia, with special reference to the December 1979 rainstorm, Canadian Geotechnical Journal, v.18, pp. 205-216. Slope data derived from British Columbia government Terrain Resource Information Management (TRIM) data.

GIS Approach to the Geologic Map of the Santa Ana 100K Quadrangle

U.S. Geological Survey,
University of California,
Riverside, California

*By D.M. Morton, R.M. Hauser,
and K.R. Ruppert*

Contact:
R.M. Hauser
scamp@ucrac1.ucr.edu

Software:
ARC/INFO Version 7.1.1
Hardware:
Sun SPARCstation 20
Plotter:
Hewlett–Packard DesignJet
2500CP
Data Source(s):
USGS Digital Line Graph and
geology from published and
unpublished maps

A geologic map of the Santa Ana 1:100,000-scale quadrangle was first compiled in analog form and released as a typical uncolored open-file geologic map. Although an extremely useful map, it had to be hand-colored for any serious use and could only be used at the publication scale. When digital capabilities became available to the Southern California Areal Mapping Project (SCAMP), a joint project of the U.S. Geological Survey and the California Division of Mines and Geology (CDMG), the Santa Ana quadrangle was redone in digital form. The resulting digital geologic map includes the most recent and largest scale geologic mapping available.

Shown here is the preliminary digital version of the Santa Ana quadrangle (USGS open-file 99-172). This preliminary release includes a read-me file, digital geological database, and a plot file that is available at http://geology.wr.usgs.gov/wgmt/scamp/scamp.html. A subsequent version, to be released on CD–ROM as well as on the Internet, will include considerably more geologic data than the geologic map. SCAMP will produce digital 4D geologic map databases that will form a digital folio series, a modern digital version of the USGS analog folio series. The folio will also include an extensive geologic base of isostatic gravity and residual magnetic maps, rock chemistry and isotopic data, and other physical property data. SCAMP has developed an exhaustive geologic data attribute coding system that will be used for the geologic databases.

To reduce potential ambiguity and produce the clearest understanding of the geology of the Santa Ana quadrangle, the folio will include numerous digital images that will show an extensive array of geologic features. Digital images will range in scale from satellite images and aerial photographs through outcrop-scale to photomicrographs; analytical data will be tied to the images. Use of digital images will produce a virtual geologic field trip at scales ranging from satellite to microscopic.

SCAMP interacts with a large number of federal, state, and local agencies as cooperators whose geologic requirements are wide-ranging and include geologic hazards, mineral resources, endangered species, groundwater recharge, contamination mitigation, utilization, and variety of environmental issues.

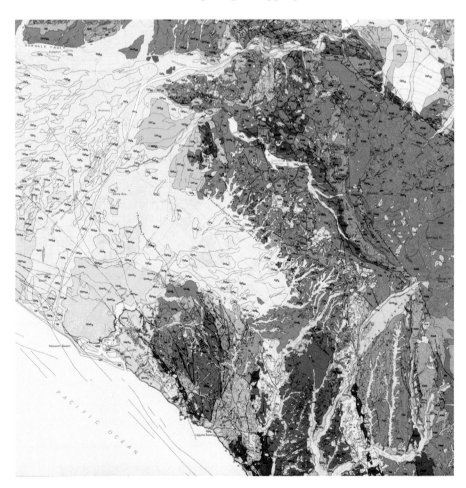

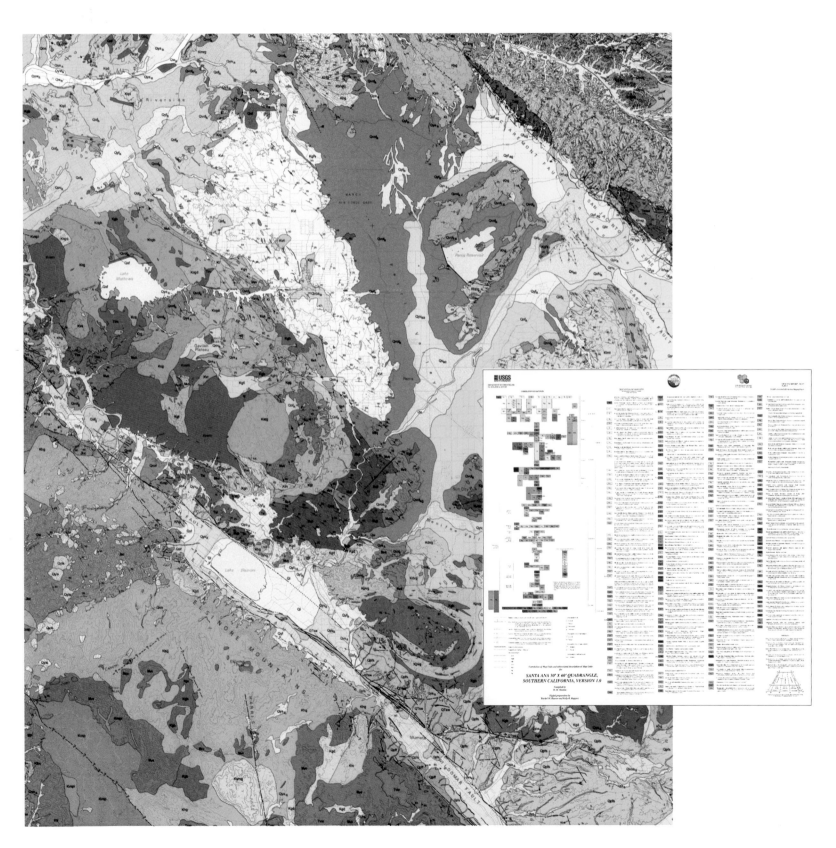

Developing Common Ecological Regions Using Major Land Resource Area Revision Through Aggregation of STATSGO-MARTHA's

National Soil Survey Center,
USDA Natural Resources
Conservation Service, Lincoln,
Nebraska

Center for International Earth
Science Information Network at
Columbia Earth Institute, Fort
Collins, Colorado

*By Sharon Waltman (NRCS) and
Vern Thomas (CIESIN)*

Contact:
Sharon Waltman
swaltman@gw.nssc.nrcs.usda.gov

Software:
ARC/INFO Version 7.1 and
ArcView GIS Version 3.1
Hardware:
Sun SPARCstation 10
Data Source(s):
Land Resource Regions and
Major Land Resource Areas of
the United States, USDA Natural
Resources Conservation
Service, National Soil Geo-
graphic database, state soil
geographic data for the United
States and Territory of Puerto
Rico

The Natural Resources Conservation Service (NRCS), in conjunction with the Center for International Earth Science Information Network (CIESIN), developed a process to revise Major Land Resource Areas (MLRA) delineation using State Soil Geographic (STATSGO) database polygon data.

In 1996, NRCS began to revise the 1984 version of MLRAs (1:7,500,000) through the aggregation of STATSGO polygon delineations (1:250,000). The main benefit of this effort is the logical linkage between two formerly separate and independently created data sets, MLRA versus STATSGO.

Working with NRCS personnel, the Active Response Geographic Information System (AR/GIS) team of CIESIN created a powerful spatial decision support system for the soil scientist using ArcView GIS and AR/GIS customized functionality. This functionality facilitates iterative reclassification of MLRA concepts according to STATSGO polygons as well as identifying data errors and misclassifications.

AR/GIS functionality includes "smart shapes" polygon reclassification capability that enables the soil scientist to quickly and efficiently reclassify STATSGO polygons. Each reclassification set can be traced with rationale files created by the soil scientist and are attached to each reclassified polygon record. The system expedites refinement of MLRA delineation using STATSGO polygons to generate a new MLRA map data set that contains new, more precise, and accurate delineations that capture soil scientist expertise, knowledge, and spatial reasoning. The system also eliminates the need for re-digitizing new MLRA lines.

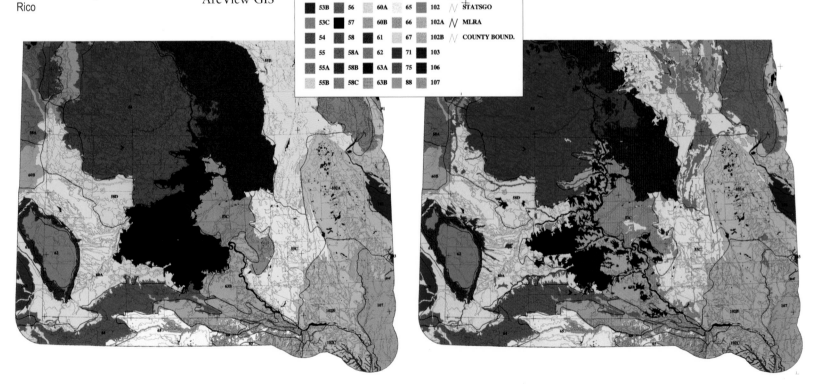

Vegetation Map of Iceland

The vegetation map of Iceland in 1:500,000 scale shows the predominant vegetation groups in simplified terms. In areas with more or less unbroken vegetation cover, the predominant form of vegetation is shown. In regions where vegetation covers half or less of the area, the type of land is indicated. Topographic information such as lakes, rivers and glaciers as well as towns and roads are also identified.

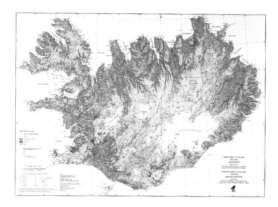

Icelandic Institute of Natural History, Reykjavik, Iceland

By Hans H. Hansen, Gudmundur Gudjonsson, and Einar Gislason

Contact:
Hans Hansen
hans@nattfs.is

Software:
ARC/INFO
Hardware:
Sun SPARCstation 20
Plotter:
Printed
Data Source(s):
Icelandic Institute of Natural History, Agricultural Research Institute, and Icelandic Forest Service

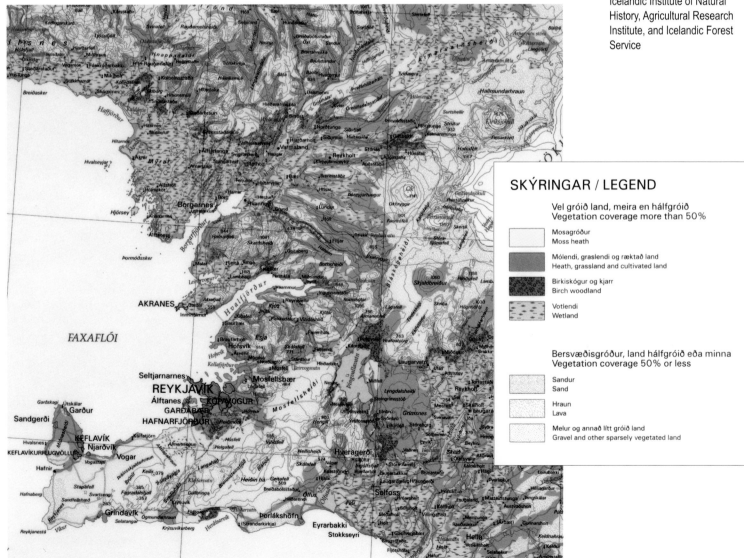

SKÝRINGAR / LEGEND

Vel gróið land, meira en hálfgróið
Vegetation coverage more than 50%

Mosagróður
Moss heath

Mólendi, graslendi og ræktað land
Heath, grassland and cultivated land

Birkiskógur og kjarr
Birch woodland

Votlendi
Wetland

Bersvæðisgróður, land hálfgróið eða minna
Vegetation coverage 50% or less

Sandur
Sand

Hraun
Lava

Melur og annað lítt gróið land
Gravel and other sparsely vegetated land

Travelers Map of Iceland

Hans H. Hansen, Reykjavik,
Iceland

*By Hans H. Hansen and
Gudmundur Hafberg*

Contact:
Hans Hansen
hans@nattfs.is

Software:
ARC/INFO
Hardware:
Windows NT
Plotter:
Printed
Data Source(s):
National Land Survey of Iceland,
Icelandic Institute of Natural
History

The travel map of Iceland in the scale of 1:600,000 is a good overview map and a must for every traveler in Iceland. It shows the country's vegetation together with hill shading. The map includes up-to-date information on the road network, campsites, swimming pools, and museums. The legend is in four languages—Icelandic, English, French, and German. On the reverse of the map are details and color photographs of Iceland's most famous attractions together with a table of road distances.

Maps of Palestine

Ministry of Planning and
International Cooperation
(MOPIC), Palestine National
Authority

*By Ministry of Planning and
Good Shepherd Engineering and
Computing*

Contact:
Bashar Iumaa
jumaa@nmopic.pna.net

Software:
ArcCAD, ArcView GIS, and
ARC/INFO
Hardware:
Hewlett–Packard workstations
Plotter:
Hewlett–Packard DesignJet 650C
Data source(s):
Local and others

The Ministry of Planning and International Cooperation (MOPIC) is one of the pioneer institutions in the Palestinian National Authority that values the importance of the role of GIS in the planning process. These maps display the process toward developing a GIS at the regional planning level to comply with the mandate of MOPIC. This will involve data transfer to other institutions working at the local planning level.

Availability of the data sources has been one of the major obstacles in building the GIS. Israeli data for the Palestinian areas were not delivered to the Palestinians according to the Oslo Agreement. Palestinian resources are old, diverse, and of different resolutions, scales, and projections. The technical data about the coordinate systems (the local grid) are Israeli classified data. Having been denied the right to buy Israeli commercial data, the tiny contour lines on this map were digitized line by line from an old British map (1934), which took more than six months to accomplish.

One of the major outputs of the planning process is the Regional Plan of the West Bank and Gaza. The Base Map of Gaza Governorates displays the current situation according to the 1994 Cairo Agreement map.

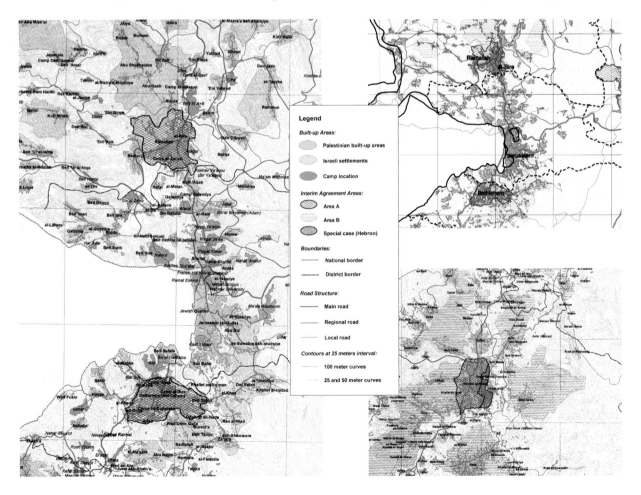

Taganrog — Planning of Boundaries of Electoral and Administrative Units

Cadastre Bureau of Taganrog,
Taganrog, Russia

By Valentin Kholodov

Software:
ARC/INFO Version 7.1.1 and
ArcView GIS Version 3.0a
Hardware:
IBM RS/6000 AIX 4.1.4, Pentium
Pro Workstation, and Windows
NT 4.0
Plotter:
CalComp 5336 GT
Data Source(s):
Municipal planning and
engineering data

This project was developed for the Municipal Election Committee of Taganrog. It involved defining the boundaries of electoral and other administrative units by voter density, preparing the pre-election campaign papers, and the graphic representation of the voting results.

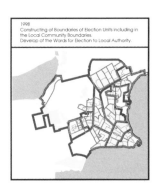

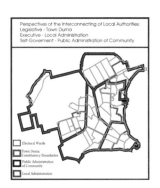

Plan of Election Ward

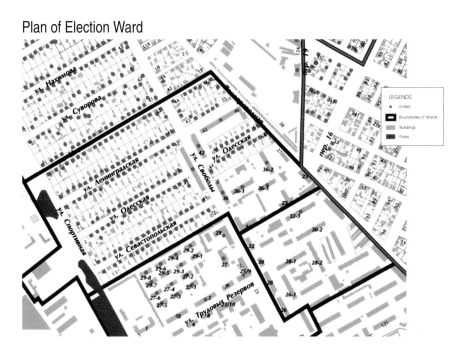

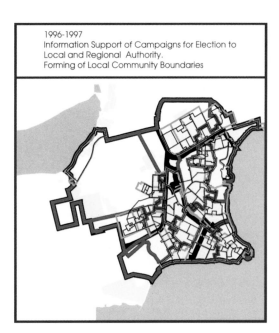

Constructing of Election Ward by A Quantity of Voters

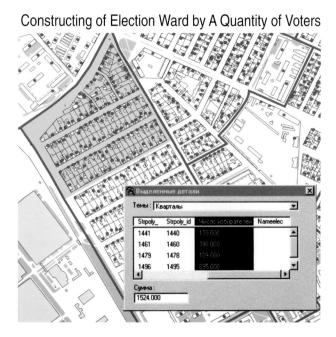

The Materials for the Deputies Election of the Ukraine, Deputies of District and Local Councils, and a Head of a Local Council

The State Research and
Production Enterprise
"Lutskmistobud," Lutsk, Ukraine

*By A. Kholodkov, V. Chirkov,
O. Ostrovetsky, O. Didovsky, and
J. Gardgala*

Contact:
A. Kholodkov,
gis@cadasr.lutsk.ua

Software:
ARC/INFO Version 3.5.1 and
ArcView GIS Version 3.0a
Hardware:
Pentium II 266
Plotter:
Hewlett–Packard DesignJet 750C
Data Source(s):
Lutsk City Statistics Board

GIS software was used to digitize existing graphic material and compile attributions for this map. Information from the Lutsk City Statistics Board database was used to divide the city into districts and create accounting allotments.

The resulting GIS maps enabled Ukrainian election deputies to successfully hold state elections for the legislative and executive branches of government.

This project also is enabling the city to develop a cadastral database. The information compiled includes topography, buildings and structures, and communications networks. Local authorities are using this information in the implementation of an economic development program.

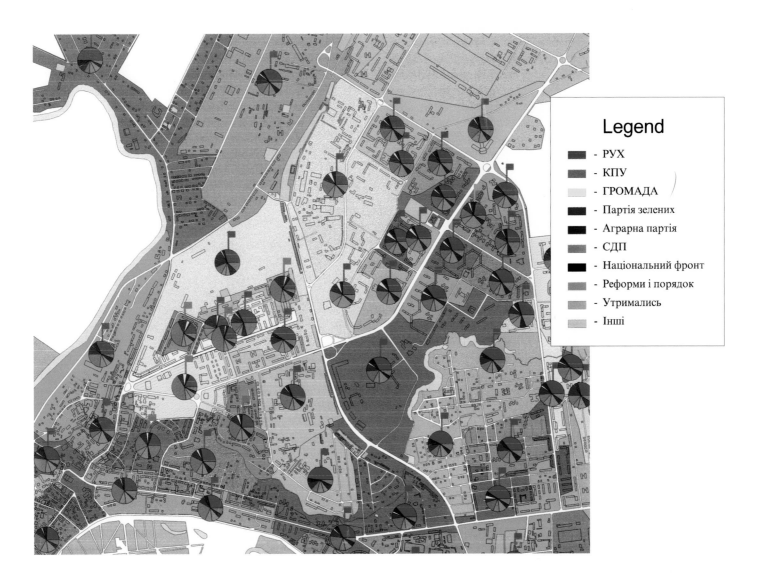

Legend
- РУХ
- КПУ
- ГРОМАДА
- Партія зелених
- Аграрна партія
- СДП
- Національний фронт
- Реформи і порядок
- Утримались
- Інші

The Status of Maternal and Child Health in Yakima County

Yakima County GIS and Yakima
Valley Memorial Hospital,
Yakima, Washington

*By Cynthia Kozma, Diane
Patterson, and Michael Vachon*

Contact:
Mike Vachon
mikev@co.yakima.wa.us

Software:
ARC/INFO Version 7.2.1
Hardware:
Hewlett–Packard D380/2
Plotter:
Canon Color Copier
Data Source(s):
Washington State Department of
Health, Birth Event records, and
Yakima County GIS database

The maternal and child population in Yakima County is diverse and geographically unique. Providing nursing services to this population requires analyzing the geographic distribution of services and their demographic characteristics. Birth records geo-coded to the census block group provide a way to assess the target population. This set of maps allows public health nurses and administrators to assure appropriate service delivery at the neighborhood level.

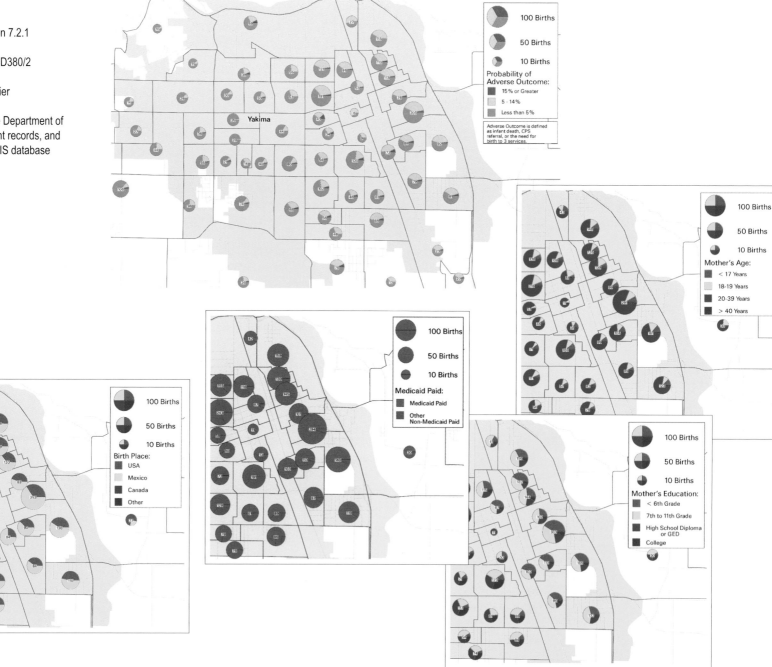

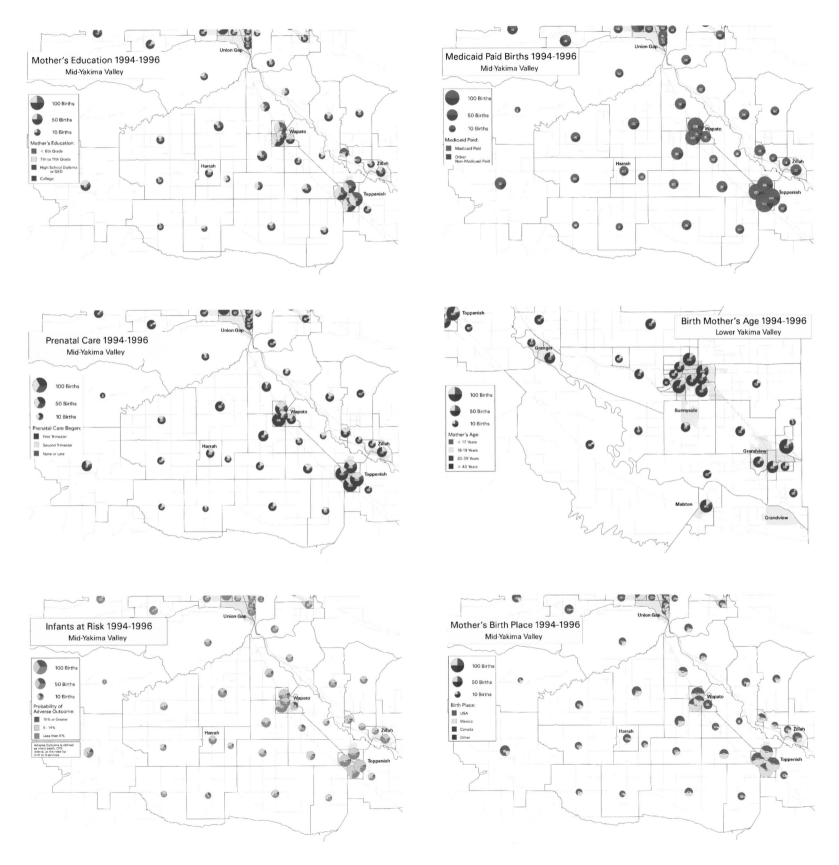

Mother's Education 1994-1996
Mid-Yakima Valley

100 Births
50 Births
10 Births

Mother's Education:
< 6th Grade
7th to 11th Grade
High School Diploma or GED
College

Medicaid Paid Births 1994-1996
Mid-Yakima Valley

100 Births
50 Births
10 Births

Medicaid Paid:
Medicaid Paid
Other Non-Medicaid Paid

Prenatal Care 1994-1996
Mid-Yakima Valley

100 Births
50 Births
10 Births

Prenatal Care Began:
First Trimester
Second Trimester
None or Late

Birth Mother's Age 1994-1996
Lower Yakima Valley

100 Births
50 Births
10 Births

Mother's Age:
< 17 Years
18-19 Years
20-39 Years
> 40 Years

Infants at Risk 1994-1996
Mid-Yakima Valley

100 Births
50 Births
10 Births

Probability of Adverse Outcome:
15% or Greater
5 - 14%
Less than 5%

Adverse Outcome is defined as infant death, CPS referral, or the need for birth to 3 services.

Mother's Birth Place 1994-1996
Mid-Yakima Valley

100 Births
50 Births
10 Births

Birth Place:
USA
Mexico
Canada
Other

Snapshots: Health and Disease Across the State

North Carolina State Center for
Health Statistics, Raleigh,
North Carolina

*By Dianne Enright and
Carol Hanchette*

Contact:
Dianne Enright
denright@gis.sches.ehnr.state.nc.us

Software:
ARC/INFO Version 7.1
Hardware:
Sun SPARCstation 20
Plotter:
Hewlett–Packard DesingJet 650C
Data Sources(s):
North Carolina State Center for
Health Statistics

These maps were developed as part of an annual vital statistics report for the state of North Carolina. They are intended to serve as a basic resource for individuals, institutions, and agencies delivering and/or planning health services for the citizens of North Carolina.

Each map shows a five-year rate for the 100 counties in North Carolina, with the exception of pregnancy, which is an annual rate.

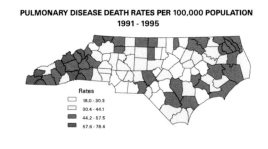

PULMONARY DISEASE DEATH RATES PER 100,000 POPULATION
1991 - 1995

Rates
18.0 - 30.3
30.4 - 44.1
44.2 - 57.5
57.6 - 78.4

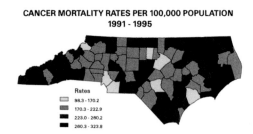

CANCER MORTALITY RATES PER 100,000 POPULATION
1991 - 1995

Rates
98.3 - 170.2
170.3 - 222.9
223.0 - 260.2
260.3 - 323.8

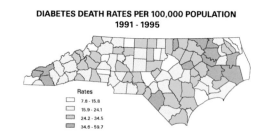

DIABETES DEATH RATES PER 100,000 POPULATION
1991 - 1995

Rates
7.8 - 15.8
15.9 - 24.1
24.2 - 34.5
34.6 - 59.7

BIRTH RATES PER 1,000 POPULATION
1991 - 1995

Rates
9.1 - 11.6
11.7 - 13.9
14.0 - 16.7
16.8 - 21.8

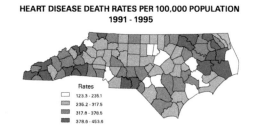

HEART DISEASE DEATH RATES PER 100,000 POPULATION
1991 - 1995

Rates
123.3 - 235.1
235.2 - 317.5
317.6 - 378.5
378.6 - 453.6

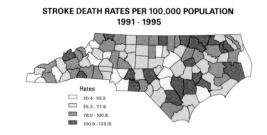

STROKE DEATH RATES PER 100,000 POPULATION
1991 - 1995

Rates
20.4 - 55.5
55.3 - 77.9
78.0 - 100.8
100.9 - 133.15

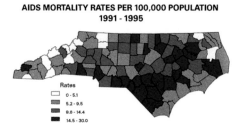

AIDS MORTALITY RATES PER 100,000 POPULATION
1991 - 1995

Rates
0 - 5.1
5.2 - 9.5
9.6 - 14.4
14.5 - 30.0

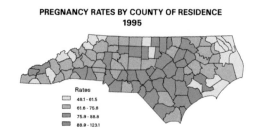

PREGNANCY RATES BY COUNTY OF RESIDENCE
1995

Rates
48.1 - 61.5
61.6 - 75.8
75.9 - 88.8
88.9 - 123.1

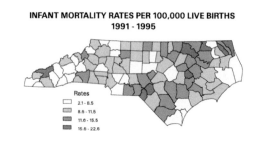

INFANT MORTALITY RATES PER 100,000 LIVE BIRTHS
1991 - 1995

Rates
2.1 - 8.5
8.6 - 11.5
11.6 - 15.5
15.6 - 22.6

Public Health National Charter of Portugal

ISEGI – New University of
Lisbon, Lisbon, Portugal

*By Ana Patuleia, Marco Painho,
and Pedro Cabral*

Contact:
Ana Patuleia
m318@isegi.unl.pt

Software:
ArcView GIS Version 3.1
Hardware:
Pentium II
Plotter:
CalComp TechJET ColorGT
Data Source(s):
INE, DGS, DGV, and DGA

The Public Health National Charter of Portugal is a computer database that helps present data in a user-friendly format. It is used as an indicator of potential problem areas in the health status of the population and/or the environment and in the performance of health services. It supports data from many sources related to public health and the environment.

Being sensitive to the needs of local geographic areas when allocating health surveillance and health services is a priority. The collection, storage, and manipulation of geographic health data and health-related information can influence the progress of health monitoring, environmental health assessment, and allocation of health resources as recognized in the European Charter on Environment and Health.

Most health information systems are not developed sufficiently to generate the data required for the planning, monitoring, and management of health services. Traditionally, most data was in tabular form, which did not facilitate accessibility to users and policy makers, particularly in the case of large amounts of desegregated numerical data.

The Charter database is more flexible than traditional ones, as it enables the user to select and, to a certain degree, adjust the presentation of data. Planners and researchers can use the maps to interpret the data.

This series of maps illustrates how GIS has enabled health administrators to make informed decisions about where to locate pharmacies, where disease outbreaks are likely to occur, and why accidents or health risks are prevalent in some areas.

Malta Fever Incidence Rate

Malta fever is a bacterial disease, it can have acute or chronic form and in some countries is considered a professional disease.

The contamination is by the ingestion of fresh cheese or infected meat, contact with secretion or other products from the animals infected, and even through dust.

Human transmission is rare and the duration of the disease is not well known. In Portugal the main foci are cows, sheep's and occasionally pigs.

To prevent this disease is fundamental to treat the milk and to eliminate all the infected animals, and that included the infected flock, and the vaccination of young animals. The problem of human infection can only be resolved throughout the elimination of infected flock.

The education is the most precious measure against the disease, so all health professionals from those areas where the Malta fever is high should be prepared for this task. (Gonçalves Ferreira, 1992)

The map illustrate the municipalities where the disease is most relevant, which more or less coincide with the regions where is raised more cattle.

Malta Fever Incidence Rate
- 0.003 - 0.203
- 0.203 - 0.45
- 0.45 - 0.845
- 0.845 - 1.705
- 1.705 - 3.158
- No Data

Data Source: DGS (1996)

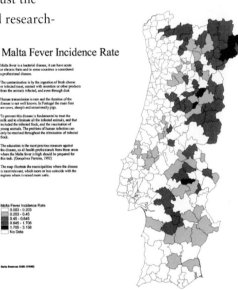

Radon (mean)

Environment can have an important influence on health, ionizing radiation from natural sources in certain circumstances can disrupt normal biological processes in living tissues. Ionizing radiation may therefore represent a health hazard to mankind. (Cliff, 1993)

Radon, a naturally occurring radioactive gas, is present everywhere on the surface of the earth. It can accumulate and reach high concentrations in buildings.

Absorbed radiation creates an increase risk of cancer (ICD 140-208 and 230-239) while irradiation of the reproductive organs may increase the risk of hereditable (genetic) damage. (Cliff, 1993)

The Radiological Protection and Safety Department in 1987 implemented a program for the evaluation of indoor radon concentrations in Portugal.

This program was started in dwellings in zones of technologically enhanced natural radioactivity and was later enlarged to the whole country. A relationship between indoor radon concentrations and the presence of granite formation is observed.

The disparities of indoor radon in the granite and non-granite regions are probably still overemphasized due to the poor ventilation of the dwellings from the granite regions, which are situated in the colder climatic zones of the country. (Teixeira, 1991)

Radon (mean) Bq m3
- 6 - 30
- 31 - 60
- 61 - 109
- 110 - 180
- 181 - 268
- No Data

Data Source: DGA (1996)

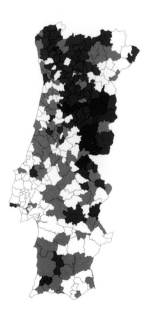

Inhab/ Pharmacy

Pharmacies in Portugal play a important role as last place (and many times as first) where patients have a last contact (or first) with healthy services.

The quality and number of these institutions is essential. To warrant the efficiency of these services the State is responsible to grant license according with some parameters for open more, never living the remaining with less than 3000 inhabitants per pharmacy.

When the ratio inhabit / Pharm. is equal or superior to 6000, the tax of Youth or Elderly is superior to 20% the conditions can be considered imperative to open another pharmacy. The municipalities highlight are the ones falling in these selection parameters.

Inhab/Pharm.
- 1583 - 2620
- 2621 - 3825
- 3826 - 5250
- 5251 - 7307
- 7308 - 10030
- No Data

Data Source: INE (1996)

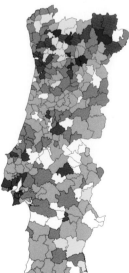

Road Accidents and Alcohol

Although transport is considered as an important part of the economy and lifestyle of contemporary Europe, it exacts a high price from society and environment.

Transport is an important source of air and water pollution and also contributes to the degradation of landscape.

Life quality in urban residents is reduced by the noise, air pollution among other factors, leading to permanent impairment of health or aggravating chronic disease.

Among the most obvious, direct health effects are deaths and injuries caused by traffic accidents. (Bertollini, 1996)

Road traffic accidents are a major drain upon the health services of the developed nations, resulting in casualties who required immediate medical attention and, frequently, long-term care.

They represent a significant burden upon any area's medical services.

The emergency procedures which have to be mobilized in the event of an accident are not only costly in their own right but, because they interrupt the normal routine of hospital and ambulance services, have a hidden opportunity cost in public health authorities.

Most of the road accidents occur within a short distance of place of occurrence and therefore within urban areas. (Cliff, 1993)

At Portugal the numbers of road accidents are almost the same since 1990, they are responsible for high mortality, deficient and morbidity ratios.

Most of the accidents involving injuries and deaths occur due to the behavior of individual conductors, that are under the effect of alcohol, drugs or didn't respect transit regulation. (DGS, 1997)

Victims
- 1 - 4
- 5 - 10
- 11 - 19
- 20 - 31
- 32 - 114
- No Data

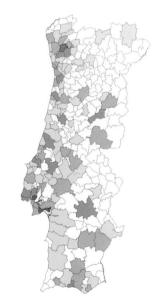

AGI Projects 1997–1998

Applied Geographics, Inc.,
Boston, Massachusetts

*By Richard Sutton, Nick Wilkoff,
David Weaver, Mike Shellito,
Pak Yen Lim, Lisa Rando,
Daniel Nvule, and Fang Yu*

Contact:
Richard Grady
grady@appgeo.com

Software:
ARC/INFO Version 7.1 and
ArcView GIS Version 3.1
Hardware:
Gateway GP6
Plotter:
Hewlett–Packard DesignJet
2500CP
Data Source(s):
MassGIS and project data

Hines Project

The location of Hines projects in relation to other real estate projects in the city—under construction, planned, and completed since 1965—are indicated on this map.

Zoning Height Classifications

This map was developed as part of a zoning analysis that was conducted for the Cambridge Community Development Department and its Citywide Growth Management Advisory Committee. In particular, the zoning analysis focused on the allowable building heights to identify potential transition zones that would minimize the height differences along zoning district borders. The map classifies the zoning districts by their allowable building heights and indicates the difference of allowable building height between adjacent districts.

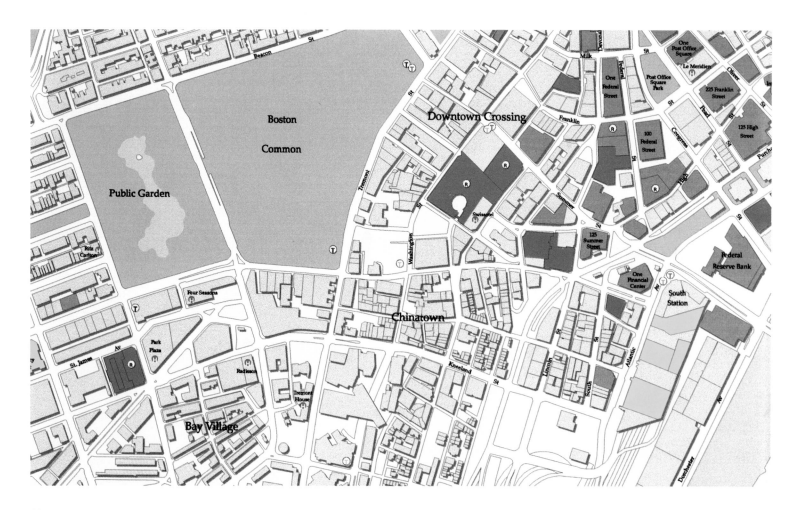

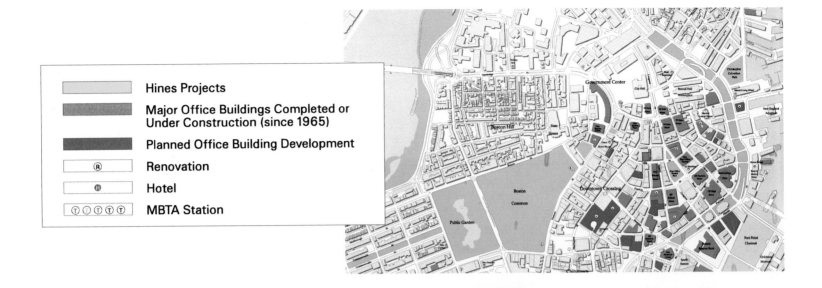

Hines Projects	
Major Office Buildings Completed or Under Construction (since 1965)	
Planned Office Building Development	
®	Renovation
Ⓗ	Hotel
Ⓣ Ⓣ Ⓣ Ⓣ	MBTA Station

Zoning Height Classifications

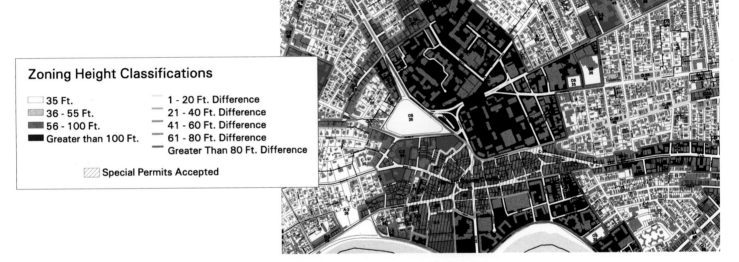

- ☐ 35 Ft.
- ▨ 36 - 55 Ft.
- ▨ 56 - 100 Ft.
- ■ Greater than 100 Ft.

- — 1 - 20 Ft. Difference
- — 21 - 40 Ft. Difference
- — 41 - 60 Ft. Difference
- — 61 - 80 Ft. Difference
- — Greater Than 80 Ft. Difference

▨ Special Permits Accepted

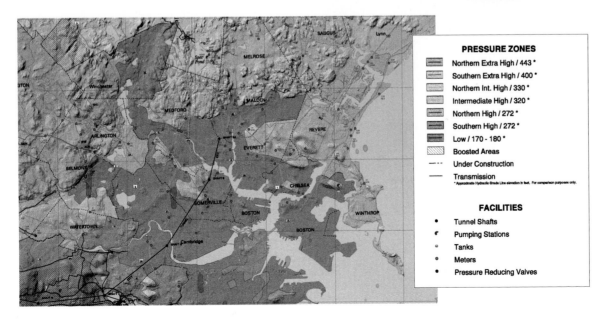

PRESSURE ZONES

- ▨ Northern Extra High / 443 *
- ▨ Southern Extra High / 400 *
- ▨ Northern Int. High / 330 *
- ▨ Intermediate High / 320 *
- ▨ Northern High / 272 *
- ▨ Southern High / 272 *
- ▨ Low / 170 - 180 *
- ▨ Boosted Areas
- --- Under Construction
- — Transmission

*Approximate Hydraulic Grade Line elevation in feet. For comparison purposes only.

FACILITIES

- • Tunnel Shafts
- ☙ Pumping Stations
- ⊙ Tanks
- • Meters
- • Pressure Reducing Valves

City of Stockton GIS Applications

MIS/GIS Department, City of
Stockton, California

*By Vince Huey and
Robert MacLeod*

Contact:
Robert MacLeod
209.937.8903

Software:
ARC/INFO Version 7.1.2,
ArcView Network Analyst, and
ArcView GIS Version 3.0
Hardware:
IBM RISC/6000
Plotter:
Hewlett–Packard DesignJet
755CM
Data Sources(s):
City of Stockton GIS database

The City of Stockton General Plan Land Use/Circulation Diagram is a visual representation of the City's policy regarding physical growth and development. The map shows present and future land uses and circulation within the city's planning area. The general plan is an example of the planning department's database, and it also includes zoning, land-use and other related planning data.

The Fire Response Times map was created for the city's fire department to model present delivery of emergency services to the community. The response time polygons were created using ArcView GIS Version 3.0 and ArcView Network Analyst. The polygons and other data layers were mapped using ARC/INFO resulting in the final map product.

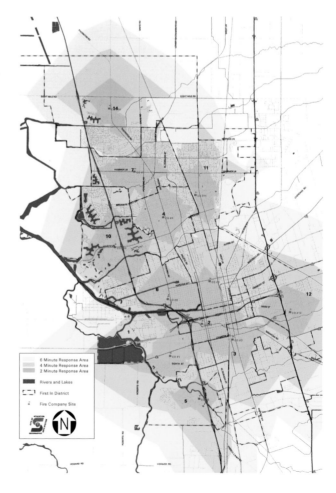

Using Multi-spectral Aerial Photography to Establish Stormwater Runoff Fees in an Urban Environment

Information Systems,
City of Salinas, California

*By Charles Lerable and
Georgia Pritchett*

Contact:
Charles Lerable
chuck@ci.salinas.ca.us

Software:
ARC/INFO Version 7.1.1,
ARC GRID, and ArcView GIS
Version 3.0
Hardware:
Sun SPARCstation 20
Plotter:
Hewlett–Packard DesignJet 3500CP
Data Source(s):
City of Salinas and Hammon,
Jensen, Wallen & Associates, Inc.

The National Pollutant Discharge Elimination System (NPDES) requires local authorities to control non-point source pollutants from entering the nation's waterways. To fund a program of compliance, Salinas, California, is considering the feasibility of charging impact fees based on storm water runoff attributed to each city parcel.

Policy direction was to develop a two-tiered fee system: a flat fee for parcels with one single-family dwelling and a fee for all other parcels based on the square footage of non-permeable surfaces. This involved isolating single family parcels from more than 26,000 parcels in the city. The city relied on its Land Use Coding System (LUCOS) to provide the necessary land use data.

Different land use classes assumed as permeable or non-permeable surfaces helped to determine soil permeability from the aerial image. An ISODATA clustering technique was used to separate spectral responses into given classes. Every pixel in the image was assigned to one of the defined classes and grouped together.

GIS processing of orthophoto-image classes involved first converting the classified images to an ARC GRID file. The ARC GRID file was converted to a polygon coverage where similar classes were grouped together into homogeneous units. This data was joined to the city's polygon parcel coverage to produce the permeable and non-permeable areas for each parcel.

The fee schedule was developed by taking the first year's monitoring and cleanup costs and allocating those costs to single-family dwellings and to all other land uses based on their total percentage of citywide non-permeable surfaces.

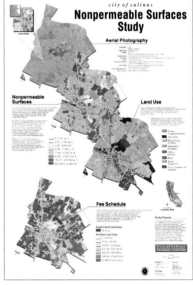

city of salinas
Nonpermeable Surfaces Study

Land Use

Policy direction was to develop a two tiered fee system: a flat fee for parcels with one single family dwelling and a fee for all other parcels based on the square footage of nonpermeable surfaces. This involved isolating single family parcels from the City's 26,000+ parcel base.

The City relied upon its Land Use Coding System (LUCOS) to provide the necessary land use data. LUCOS classifies all land uses into thirty-four land use categories. This coding system has been grouped into the general land use categories shown below.

- Vacant/ Vacant Developed
- Agriculture
- Single Family Dwelling
- Multifamily Dwellings
- Offices/ Services
- Retail
- Public/ Semipublic
- Heavy Commercial/ Industrial

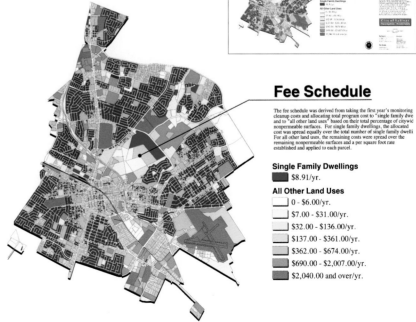

Fee Schedule

The fee schedule was derived from taking the first year's monitoring cleanup costs and allocating total program cost to "single family dwe and to "all other land uses" based on their total percentage of citywide nonpermeable surfaces. For single family dwellings, the allocated cost was spread equally over the total number of single family dwelli For all other land uses, the remaining costs were spread over the remaining nonpermeable surfaces and a per square foot rate established and applied to each parcel.

Single Family Dwellings
- $8.91/yr.

All Other Land Uses
- 0 - $6.00/yr.
- $7.00 - $31.00/yr.
- $32.00 - $136.00/yr.
- $137.00 - $361.00/yr.
- $362.00 - $674.00/yr.
- $690.00 - $2,007.00/yr.
- $2,040.00 and over/yr.

3-D View of King County

King County Department of
Transportation, Road Services
Division, Renton, Washington

By Victor W. High

Contact:
Victor High
victor.high@metrokc.gov

Software:
ARC/INFO Version 7.1.2,
ARC TIN, and ARC GRID
Hardware:
Sun UltraSPARC 30
Plotter:
Hewlett–Packard DesignJet 650C
Data Source(s):
USGS and King County
Information and Telecommunica-
tions Services

This map is a combination of three digital elevation models (DEM) of different scales layered on top of each other. The mountains outside of King County are a USGS 1:250,000-scale DEM. The map of the county is a USGS 1:24,000-scale DEM, and the Puget Sound DEM is from a varying resolution point coverage.

All three grids were divided into elevation colors, then an aspect grid was combined to create shadows and highlights. The point of view is a traditional one looking from downtown Seattle toward Mount Rainier. Mount Adams and Mount Saint Helens can also be seen in the background.

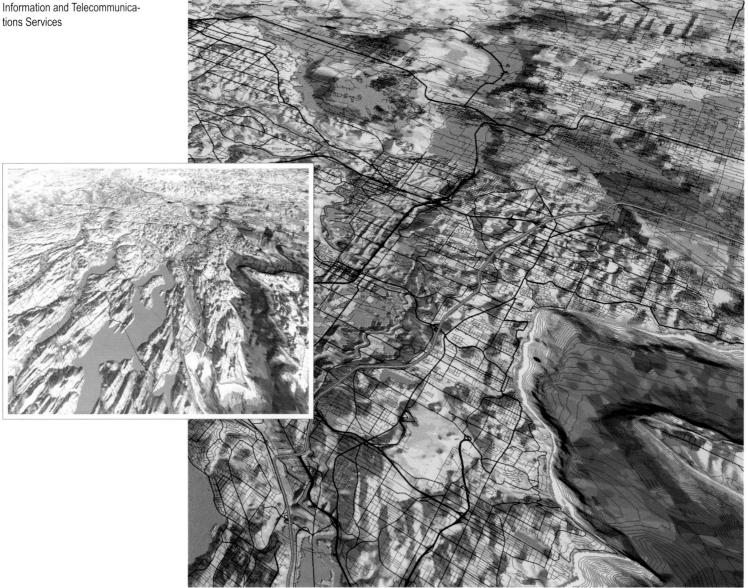

Holms Point, Inglewood, Kingsgate Area — Wetland and Stream Sensitive Roads with RNIS Drainage Data

King County Department of Transportation, Road Services Division, Renton, Washington

By Victor W. High

Contact:
Victor High
victor.high@metrokc.gov

Software:
ARC/INFO Version 7.1.1, ARC TIN, and ARC GRID
Hardware:
Sun UltraSPARC 30
Plotter:
Hewlett–Packard DesignJet 650C
Data Source(s):
USGS, King County Roads Maintenance, King County Information and Telecommunications Services, and Washington State Department of Natural Resources

This map is a graphic representation of King County's Road Network Inventory System (RNIS) overlaid onto wetland and stream buffers to show the number and types of drainage features maintained by King County Roads, their condition and proximity to environmentally sensitive areas, and the topographic elevation of the study area.

The dynamic segmentation routing module was used to place coded drainage features with linear and point measurements onto a modified TIGER street file, the King County Street Network (KCSN), dated 1996. Buffers, clip, identity and union were used on stream, lake, wetland, and road coverages to determine sensitive area acreage and sensitive road miles per gradual buffer distances.

ARC/INFO modules ARC TIN and ARC GRID were used for hill shading and surface modeling with vertical exaggeration of 2X.

King County

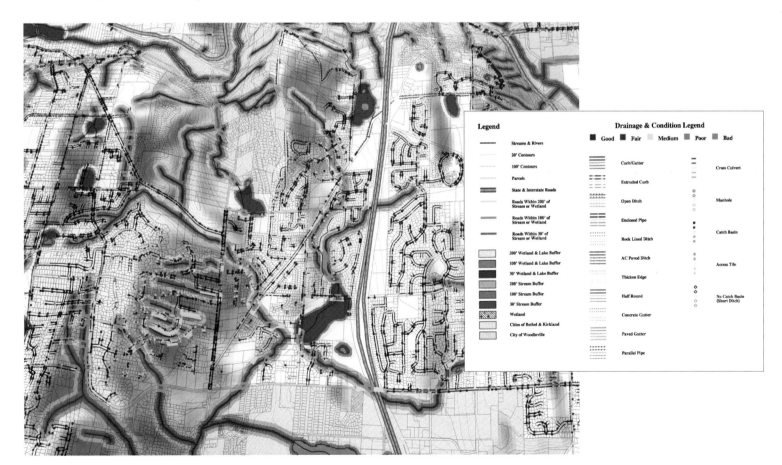

Confronting the Child Care Challenge

Kern County Superintendent of
Schools, Research Services,
Bakersfield, California

*By Adam Cabrera, Sam Tang,
and Kimberley Silva*

Contact:
Adam Cabrera
adcabrera@kern.org

Software:
ArcView GIS Version 3.0a
Hardware:
Hewlett–Packard Vectra
workstation
Plotter:
CalComp TechJET GT/PS
Data Source(s):
Department of Human Services
AFDC database and Community
Connection of Child Care
Carefinder database

To uncover gaps in child care services this map examines the distribution of CalWORKs children in relation to licensed child care providers in Bakersfield, California. Instead of using ZIP codes, which are not proportional in size and population, the data was analyzed using a method of densities per square mile. This level of analysis provided a much better representation of the need.

The following maps examine the distribution of CalWORKs children of Metro Bakersfield, Kern County. The issue here concerns two Bakersfield communities in the 93305 and 93307 ZIP code areas. When summarizing only ZIP codes, 93305 has 4,357 children while 93307 has a total (viewed portion only) of 5,752 children. These numbers can be very misleading when ZIP codes are the only method used. The estimated area of 93305 is seven square miles while the viewable area of 93307 is approximately 80 square miles. This

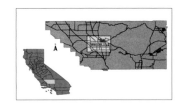

explains the higher concentration of CalWORKs children per square mile in the 93305 ZIP code.

In this and many other cases in Kern County, the use of ZIP codes and census geography is not an accurate method to determine distribution because they are not proportional in size, and therefore skew the data.

Ethical research is the foundation of any research project from the point of data collection to its final analysis and disclosure of its findings. As technology progresses in today's society, new guidelines and questions emerge regarding ethics in research especially in a GIS.

Due to the social stigma surrounding welfare and poverty, any welfare reform research must take into account the issue of anonymity and safeguard against invasion of privacy. This mapping project relied on the use of CalWORKs recipients' addresses, which poses the risk that the public could identify any CalWORKs child from the map. In an attempt to address this ethical concern, Research Services chose to use population concentrations rather than individual addresses. This technique removes the ability to recognize the sample and ensures that a subject's identity will not become public knowledge.

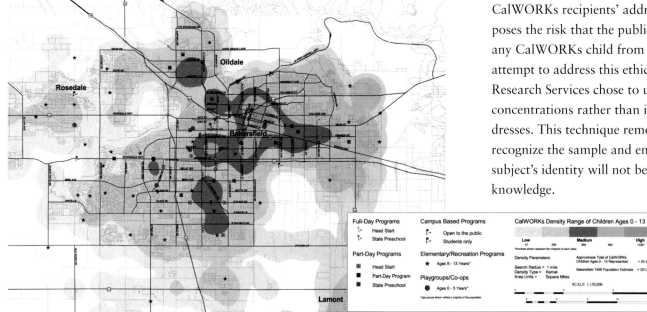

How Tax Rate Areas Are Formed

San Diego County Assessor,
San Diego, California

By Robert Short

Contact:
Robert Short
rshortas@co.san-diego.ca.us

Software:
ArcView GIS
Hardware:
Hewlett–Packard Kayak XU-
Pentium II
Plotter:
Hewlett–Packard DesignJet
2500CP
Data Source(s):
San Diego Geographic
Information Source (SanGIS)

Tax Rate Areas (TRAs) in San Diego County, California, are formed using the boundaries of districts and service areas. This plot illustrates the relationship between TRAs and districts. The map portion shows how TRAs are formed by overlaying the districts that provide services to an area. This creates areas wherein the various rates are uniform and determines the agencies for which the taxes are levied, the TRA. ArcView GIS shapefiles of TRAs, cities, community colleges, fire districts, redevelopment areas, sanitation districts, and water/irrigation districts were retrieved from the SanGIS data warehouse.

The tabular portion shows how the revenue collected from property taxes is distributed to the districts using the TRAs. These are database files generated from the TRA index, which is a file shared by the county auditor and county assessor. The files are cross-referenced to show all the districts within a TRA and to show all the TRAs that are within a district.

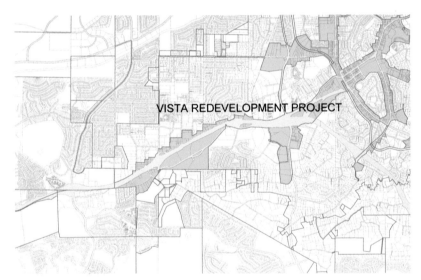

Seq	Districts in TRA 12004	Dollars per Hundrad
1	County General	15.02094
3	Greater San Diego Co. Res Conservation Dist Lan	0.00959
4	Unified Vista	42.80402
5	Palomar Community College	6.02376
6	County School Service	0.71443
7	County School Service-Capital Outlay	0.18004
8	Trainable Mentally Retarded Minors Elem Comp	0.20444
9	Physically Handicapped Minors Elem Comp	0.31570
10	Childrens Institutions Tuition	0.15231
11	Regional Occupational Centers	0.45565
12	Trainable Mentally Retarded Minors High School Comp	0.20550
13	Physically Handicapped Minors High School Comp	0.31663
14	Vista Project (19/85701)	0.01812
15	Oceanside Project (19/85001)	0.00972
16	Autistic Pupils Minors Elem Comp	0.00972
17	Carlsbad Project (19/86001).	0.00900
18	Autistic Pupils Minors High School Comp	0.00960
19	Development Centers for Handicapped EC56811 Elem	0.04482
20	Development Centers for Handicapped EC56811 High	0.04611
21	Educational Revenue Augmentation Fund	14.68024
22	Vista City	14.62024
23	Tri City Hospital District Maint	1.88637
24	Vista Irrigation- Lan	0.37432
2	County Library	1.34987
25	CWA Vista Irrigation	0.33876

Turning Spatial Data into Knowledge

EarthData International of NM,
Albuquerque, New Mexico

*By Michael Brandt and
Robert Sours*

Contact:
Patty Pringle–Roberts
proberts@earthdata.com

Software:
ARC/INFO and ArcView GIS
Hardware:
UNIX and PC workstations
Plotter:
Hewlett–Packard DesignJet
2500CP
Data Source(s):
Digital orthophotography and
existing parcel database

The City of Rio Rancho, New Mexico, obtained the services of EarthData International of NM to produce digital orthophotography for use as base mapping by their GIS department.

True color aerial photography was taken at a photo scale of 1:12,000 with a ground pixel resolution of 1.2 feet. Using soft-copy photogrammetric methods, the planimetric data was captured for buildings, edge of road, and drainage.

A ten-foot contour interval was also developed using digital terrain model (DTM) techniques. The planimetric and contour features were exported to ARC/INFO coverages so the City of Rio Rancho could develop a new GIS system. Existing right-of-way and parcel data was also rubber sheeted to the digital orthophoto base.

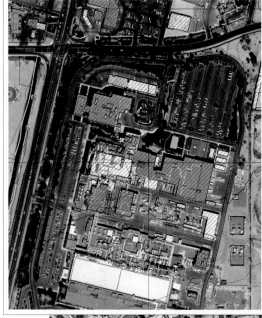

Maricopa County Regional Map and Maricopa County Supervisorial District Map

Maricopa County Department of Transportation, Phoenix, Arizona

By Tony Renaud, Larry Wolfson, Karen Stewart, Glenn Emanuel, and Will Gardner

Contact:
Larry Wolfson
larrywolfson@mail.maricopa.gov

Software:
ARCPLOT
Hardware:
Sun UltraSPARC
Plotter:
Xerox 58bo
Data Source(s):
MC DOT coverages, digital camera images, and MC FCD water coverages

The Maricopa County Department of Transportation (MC DOT) primarily plans, designs, constructs, and maintains roadways within the unincorporated areas of the county. The Regional Map is a public service map, given free of charge to any citizen.

The Supervisorial Map and Capital Improvements Program Project provides contact information for the county supervisors, and this information is mailed to constituents.

The AZTech Intelligent Transportation System (ITS) Model Deployment Initiative is a seven-year project that will develop an integrated ITS for the Phoenix metropolitan area. It is designed to produce freeway and arterial street networks that are safer and more efficient for the traveling public, decreasing travel time and enhancing traveler mobility. This project also applies a regional approach to mass transit, enabling bus drivers to transmit their location to information centers keeping travelers updated on bus schedules.

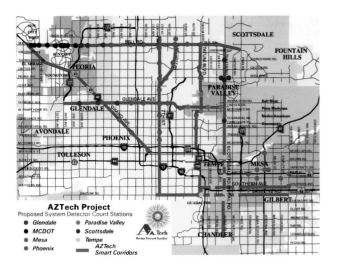

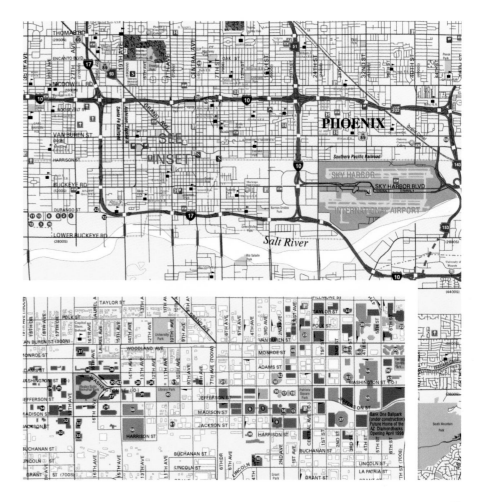

The Tacoma Dome Area Land Use

Economic Development
Department, Tacoma,
Washington

*By Mike Murnane and
Donna Wendt*

Contact:
Donna Wendt
dwendt@ci.tacoma.wa.us

Software:
ARC/INFO Version 7.1.2,
ArcView GIS Version 3.0a, and
ArcPress
Hardware:
Sun SPARCstation 10 and
Gateway E3110
Plotter:
Hewlett–Packard DesignJet
755CM
Data Source(s):
City of Tacoma

The Sound Transit project, approved by voters from a three-county area, will develop commuter rail, light rail, and additional freeway high occupancy vehicle (HOV) lanes to reduce traffic congestion in central Puget Sound.

The Tacoma Dome Area Land Use map provides necessary background and neighborhood information in the light rail/commuter rail development area.

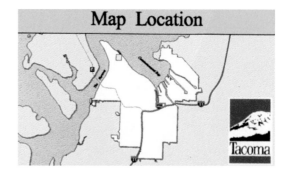

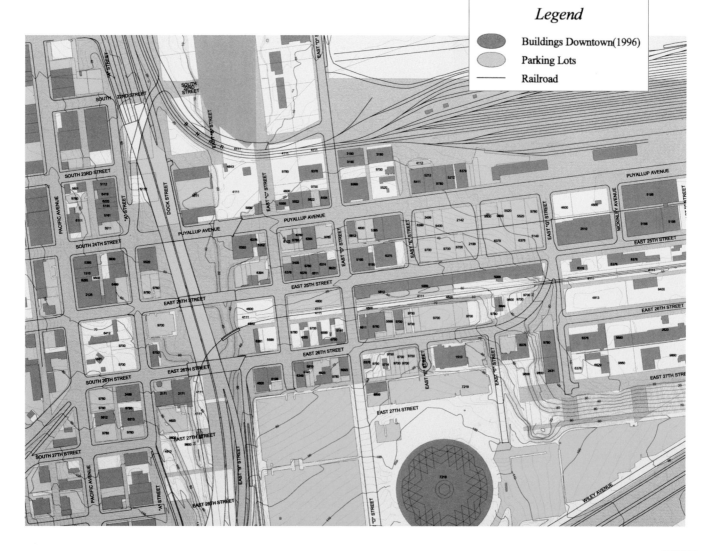

"The Sounder" Dome Station to Lakewood Connection

"The Sounder" Dome Station to Lakewood Connection identifies different options for the commuter rail connections between Tacoma and Lakewood. The commuter rail line will extend to the communities of Puyallup, Seattle, and Everett.

Tacoma Dome Area, Land Use Economic Development Department, Tacoma, Washington

By Mike Murnane and Donna Wendt

Contact:
Donna Wendt
dwendt@ci.tacoma.wa.us

Software:
ARC/INFO Version 7.1.2, ArcView GIS Version 3.0a, and ArcPress
Hardware:
Sun SPARCstation 10 and Gateway E3110
Plotter:
Hewlett–Packard DesignJet 755CM
Data Source(s):
City of Tacoma

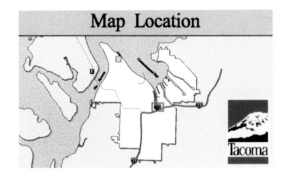

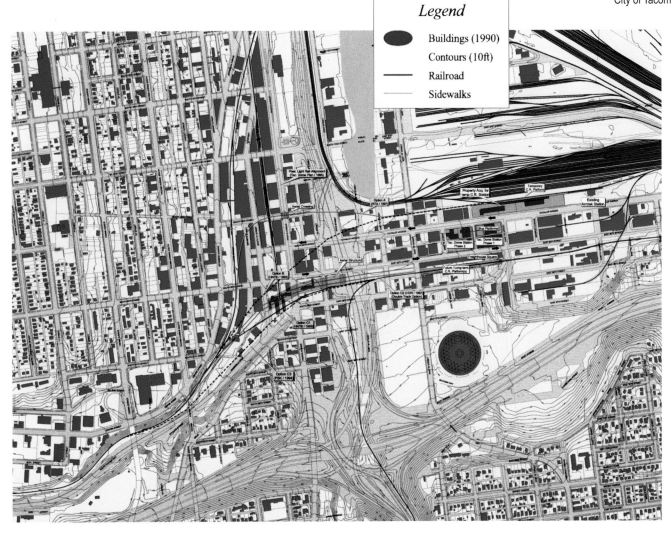

Thematic Shaded Relief Mapping

City of Johnson City, Tennessee

*By Gregory Plumb and
Ann Howland*

Contact:
Gregory Plumb
plumbg@xtn.net

Software:
ARC/INFO
Hardware:
Windows NT workstation
Plotter Used:
Hewlett–Packard DesignJet 650C
Data Source(s):
City of Johnson City and USGS

This street map of Johnson City, Jonesborough, and surrounding areas in Tennessee was produced on a shaded relief background. This version differs from black-and-white shaded relief in that color is used to symbolize areas of interest while maintaining the visualization of relief. This is achieved by implementing a hue-saturation-value (hsv) color model with three raster data layers. One of the many applications of shaded relief is its use as a base map as seen on this map.

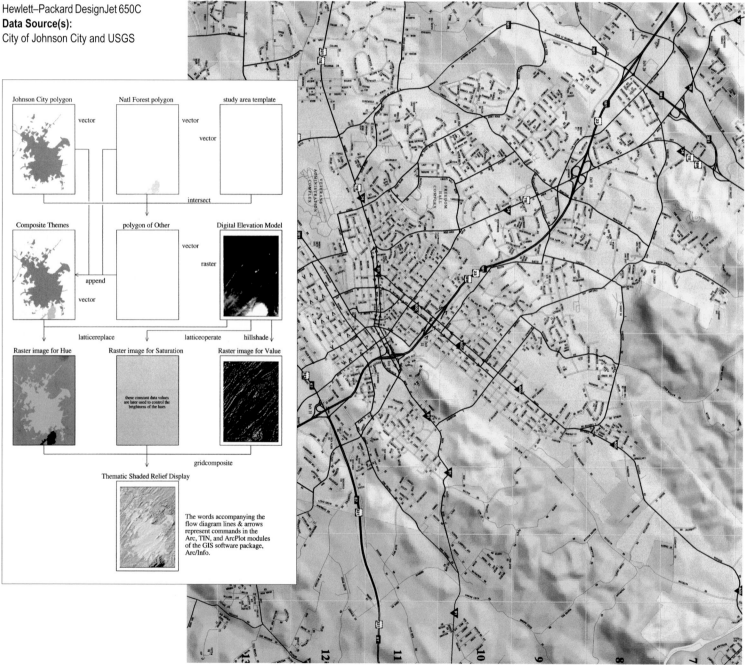

Washington County Cartography — Anatomy of a Digital Assessors Map

Washington County
Cartography, Hillsboro, Oregon

*By Jon Greninger and
Roger Livingston*

Contact:
Roger Livingston
roger_livingston@co.washington.or.us

Software:
ARC/INFO Version 7.1.1
Hardware:
Hewlett–Packard UNIX server
Plotter:
Hewlett–Packard DesignJet 750C
Data Source(s):
Recorded plats, surveys, and
deed records from Washington
County

The Assessors Map and tax lot base coverage is the foundation for all of Washington County's GIS applications. In 1996, Washington County Cartography initiated a six-year program to develop new digital assessor maps encompassing the Urban Growth Boundary throughout Washington County. The result of this project will produce one seamless tax lot boundary coverage with plus or minus one-half foot accuracy that would replace the existing county base map.

Each map is comprised of three coverages. One contains only tax lot lines, one contains only subdivision boundaries, and one easement coverage contains all other arcs to be incorporated into the map. All arcs contain specific attribute information, such as angle, distance, radius, delta, tangent arc length, and "cogosource" values, obtained from recorded plats, surveys, or other documentation.

All tax lot labels contain 12 digits. The first seven digits represent the map number and the last five digits represent the tax lot number. The new digital assessors maps are 18 inches by 24 inches and are printed on paper, while the old Mylar maps were hand-drawn on 18-inch-by-20-inch sheets.

The Meadows

City of Las Vegas, Nevada

By Christopher LaMay

Contact:
Christopher LaMay
clamay@ci.las-vegas.nv.us

Software:
ARC/INFO
Hardware:
Sun SPARCstation20/UNIX
Plotter:
Hewlett–Packard DesignJet
755CM
Data Source(s):
City and valley entities

The Las Vegas (Meadows) Valley map includes Las Vegas, North Las Vegas, Henderson, Boulder City, Clark County, major streets, freeways, airports, and Nellis AFB. The Meadows title comes from the English translation of the Spanish name Las Vegas. Clark County and the four cities funded a regional study by the Urban Land Institute, and this map was created to provide participants with a common reference map.

Originally designed without the benefit of the dramatic TIN of the valley topology, the map size was determined by the one-mile buffer around the cities and the use of a one inch = one mile scale. With the addition of the TIN, the reality of living in a valley surrounded by mountains leaps off the page.

The Meadows map has proven to be very popular with city staff and the public by providing an up-to-date, comprehensive, eye pleasing overview of the Las Vegas Valley.

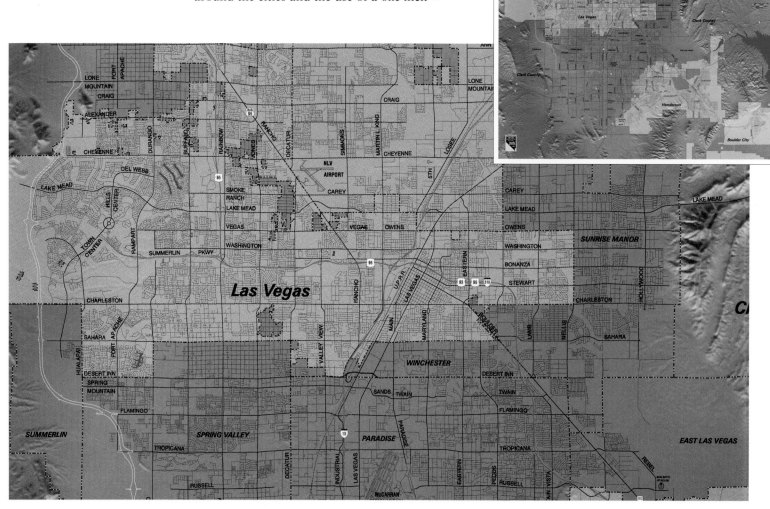

Analyzing Parcel Sale Trends in Qatar Using GIS

The Real Estate Registration Department (RERD), Ministry of Justice, State of Qatar

By Mohamed Abdul Wahab Hamouda, Naazim C. Abdullah, and Thufail Ahmad

Contact:
N. Balamohan
nbala@gisqatar.org.qa

Software:
ARC/INFO Version 7.0.1
Hardware:
DEC Alpha 2100 server
Plotter:
Hewlett–Packard DesignJet 750C
Data Source(s):
Cadastral database of RERD, Land Marks coverage of the Ministry of Interior, and the topographic database of the Center for GIS

This map depicts the trends of parcel sale transactions in Qatar. It shows the incidence/repetition of sale transactions for parcels in central Doha as they relate to the proximity of main roads, health centers, shopping areas, schools, post offices, and banks.

Legend

School		Petrol Station	
Medical Facility		Club	
Shopping Centre		No Sale Transactions	
Bank		2 - 3 Sale Transactions	
Post Office		4 - 7 Sale Transactions	
Hotel		> 7 Sale Transactions	
Mosque		Main Road	

Tactical Decision Aids

U.S. Army Topographic
Engineering Center, Alexandria,
Virginia

*By D. Visone, L. Graff,
J. Hanson, and C. Jordan*

Contact:
Daniel Visone
dvisone@tec.army.mil

Software:
ARC/INFO Version 7.1.2
Hardware:
Sun SPARCstation 20
Plotter:
Hewlett–Packard DesignJet 755
Data Sources(s):
Integrated Meteorological
System (IMETS)

These four Tactical Decisions Aids (TDAs) were generated on the Digital Topographic Support System (DTSS). The DTSS is the U.S. Army's field automated terrain analysis system that supports the commander during the Intelligence Preparation of the Battlefield (IPB) process.

The DTSS leverages off state-of-the-art, commercial, off-the-shelf technology, ARC/INFO, and ERDAS IMAGINE for database generation, spatial modeling, and image processing. Using National Imagery and Mapping Agency (NIMA) data or other sources, the system can generate TDAs to depict mobility, line-of-sight, hydrology, weather, and user-defined (Helicopter Landing Zones) analyses.

The four TDAs depicted here were created by contouring real-time weather information received from the U.S. Army's battlefield weather system, IMETS.

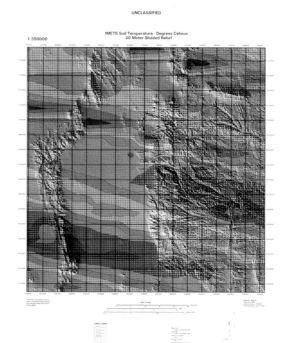

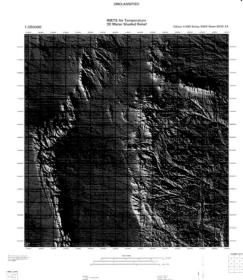

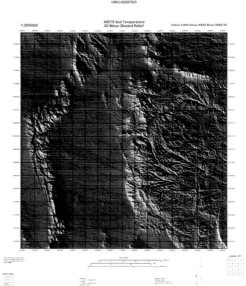

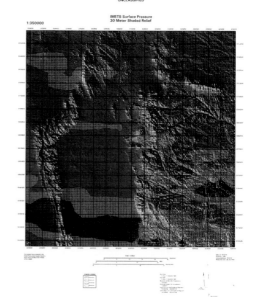

Standard Topographic Map at 1:50,000 Scale Based on GIS Vector Database DMU25

The Military Topographic Institute provides the army of the Czech Republic with topographic data. In 1994, the institute began using GIS to build the DMU25 database, which covers more than 70,000 square kilometers – the entire territory of the Czech Republic. The vector database stores graphic information in 20 coverages with a common attribute table.

Applications designed by ARC Macro Language (AML) produce 1:25,000 and 1:50,000 topographic maps from the vector data. The process of generating the maps consists of four steps. First, data is selected from the DMU25 database. Map content reduction and feature displacement involves selecting features for the map and simplifying their shapes to relate to the map scale. Finally, appropriate cartographic symbolization and annotation are performed automatically by the system, which places them into the final map product.

A graphic file is created for plotting or a Postscript file is used to generate film in a laser image setter. The final stage is offset printing.

Military Topographic Institute, Dobruska, Czech Republic

By Zdenek Martinec and Jiri Faigl

Contact:
Zdenek Martinec
zdenek.martinec@vtopu.army.cz

Software:
ARC/INFO Version 7.0.3 and AML
Hardware:
Hewlett–Packard 715/400
Data Source(s):
GIS vector database DMU25

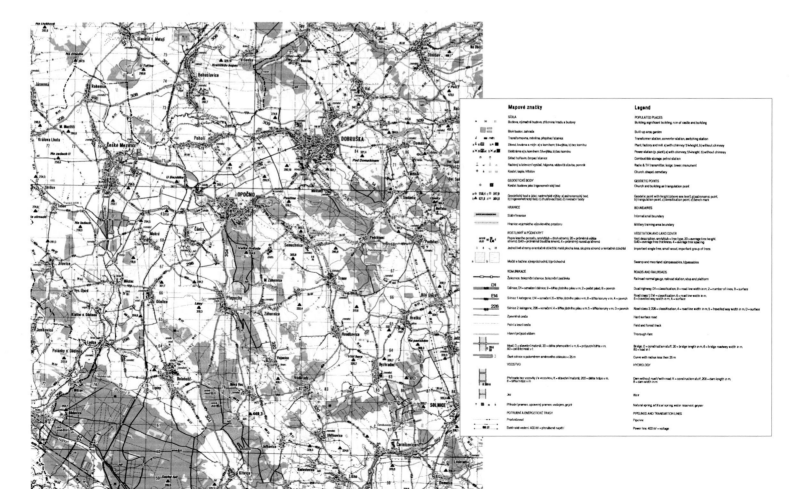

Vegetation of Michigan Circa 1800: An Interpretation of the General Land Office Surveys

Michigan Natural Features
Inventory, Lansing, Michigan

*By P.J. Comer, D.A. Albert, and
M.B. Austin*

Contact:
M.B. Austin
austinmb@state.mi.us

Software:
ARC/INFO Version 7.1.2 and
ArcView GIS Version 3.0a
Hardware:
Dell Pentium PC with Windows
NT Version 4
Plotter:
Hewlett–Packard DesignJet 650C
Data Source(s):
An Interpretation of the General
Land Office Surveys 1816 to
1856

Long-term efforts to protect and restore the water quality of the Great Lakes have evolved from primary attention on control of pollutants to maintenance and restoration of ecological integrity of the entire basin. Biological diversity, or "biodiversity" for short, refers to the array of life forms and ecological processes that support and sustain them at all levels of organization, from genetic diversity through ecosystem diversity. As land managers and conservationists grapple with how to "save all the pieces" of biodiversity, awareness is growing so that large-scale planning, at the watershed or eco-regional level, is necessary to adequately protect sustaining ecological processes. This project sought to add a valuable tool for such initiatives, a methodology for assessing this fundamental measure of ecological integrity, biodiversity.

Vegetation of Michigan Circa 1800

Basic to understanding nature is an appreciation for the relative composition and spatial pattern of vegetation across the surface of the land. Knowledge of the composition and ecological context of Michigan's vegetation, as it appeared just before rapid and widespread European–American settlement and industrialization in the 1800s, provides an important and useful point of reference.

Vegetative patterns from this period largely reflect gradually changing climate and human land use over the preceding two to five thousand years. Additionally, by comparing this information with that from more recent periods, the relatively rapid, widespread changes of the past two centuries can be easily assessed. This historical vegetation map therefore provides an important reference point for understanding cumulative impacts to natural systems caused by fragmentation and conversion. Present patterns of species distribution and ecosystem function become more meaningful when placed in this historical context.

Between 1816 and 1856, Michigan's Lower Peninsula was systematically surveyed by the General Land Office (GLO), which had been established by the federal government in 1785. Surveyors took detailed notes on the location, species, and diameter of each tree used to mark section lines and section corners. They commented on the locations of rivers, lakes, wetlands, the agricultural potential of soils, and general quality of timber along each section line as they were measured out.

Ecologists at the Michigan Natural Features Inventory developed a methodology to transfer and interpret the notes of the GLO surveys into a detailed digital map for use by researchers, land managers, and the public. The methodology for producing the map involved plotting the section-line information onto USGS topographic maps. The primary information sources for vegetation-type boundaries were topographic features, wetland information, elevation lines, dominant tree species, and the descriptive comments from the surveyors. Surface geology maps, soil maps, and other early vegetation maps were also used as secondary sources. Vegetation units smaller than 20 acres were not included on the map. Eighty-four different vegetation types were established using existing knowledge of Michigan's planned communities.

The map set (lower and upper peninsulas) is available from the Michigan Natural Features Inventory, Mason Building, Box 30444, Lansing, Michigan 48909-7944. Users of the maps should be aware that they represent an approximation of the native landscape limited by the available information.

NIWA Miscellaneous Chart Series

National Institute of Water and
Atmospheric Research Ltd.
(NIWA), Wellington,
New Zealand

*By Richard Garlick and
Lionel Carter*

Contact:
Richard Garlick
rgarlick@niwa.cri.nz

Software:
ARC/INFO Version 7.1.2
Hardware:
Sun UltraSPARC
Plotter:
Hewlett–Packard 2500
Data Sources(s):
NIWA marine database

Ocean Circulation New Zealand (opposite page)
New Zealand occupies an important position in the world ocean as the Pacific gateway for the largest deep western boundary current and the globe-encircling Antarctic circumpolar current.

This map shows surface and ocean currents around the New Zealand region and how they interact with the physiography of the New Zealand continental landmass. Although it is aimed at the public, the map is specifically targeted for schoolchildren who will receive it, along with a resource kit, as part of a program highlighting the "International Year of the Ocean."

Kaikoura Canyon: Depths, Shelf Texture, and Whale Dives (below)

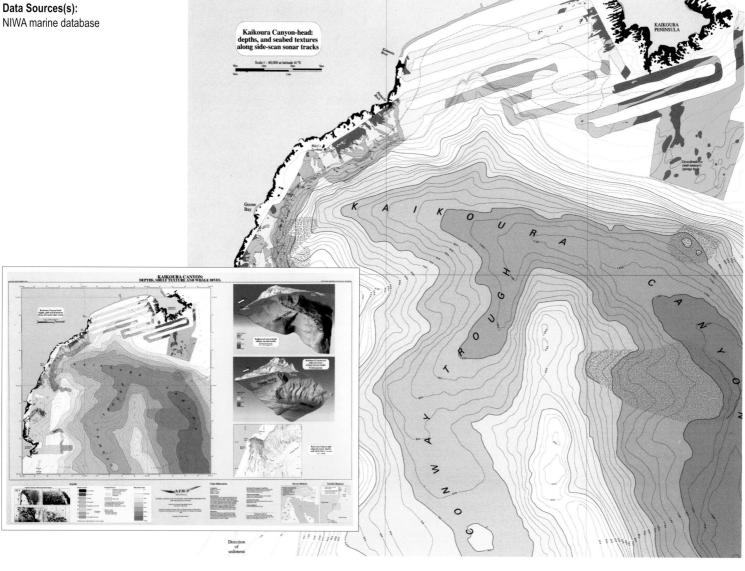

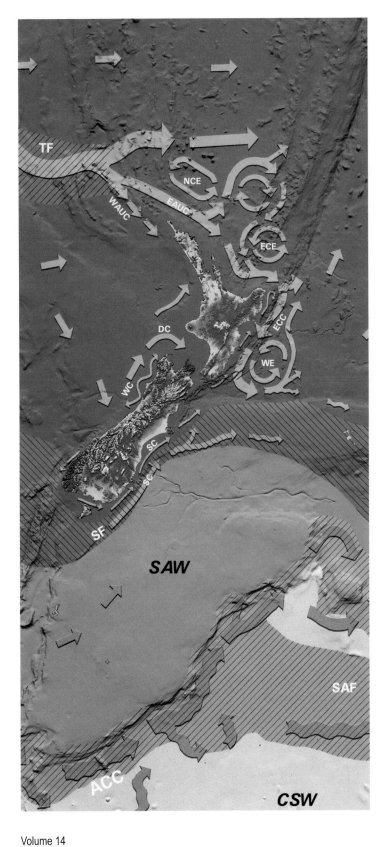

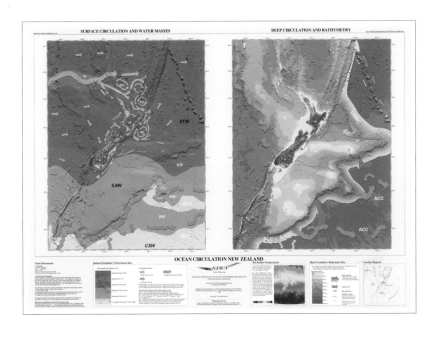

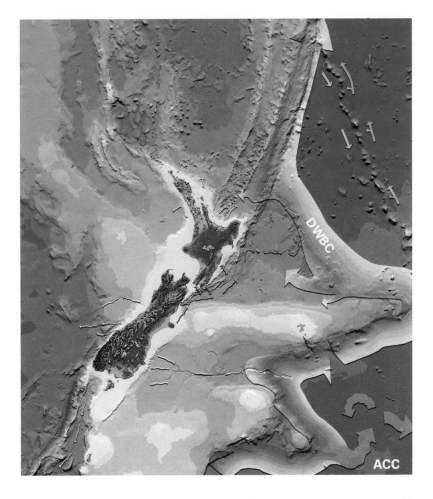

Significant Hazard Alert, Central Gulf of Mexico

United States Department of the Interior, Minerals Management Service, Gulf of Mexico OCS Region, New Orleans, Louisiana

By Jun Wu, Patrick Thorsell, Adnan Ahmed, Michele Aurand, Ralanda Camper, Leonard Coats, Michele Daigle, Holly Houston, Kewen Huang, Xueqiao Huang, Kun Li, Walter Nijak, Paul Rasmus, Linda Tedrow, Alexandra Wigle, and Yehog Zhong

Contact:
Jun Wu
jun_wu@mms.gov

Software:
ARC/INFO Version 7.0.4, ARC GRID, ArcView GIS Version 3.08, and SDE
Hardware:
Sun SPARCstations and IBM PC
Plotter:
Hewlett–Packard DesignJet 650C
Data Source(s):
MMS and NOAA

Mineral resource exploration in the Gulf of Mexico has been moving toward deepwater areas beyond the 800-meter water line. The Significant Hazard Alert shows the reported water flow and the waste dumping locations. The Hazard Alert announcement made by Minerals Management Service, U.S. Department of the Interior, is available to the public so that interested companies can evaluate their exploration and make drilling plans accordingly.

The Outer Continental Shelf (OCS) lease information in the Technical Information Management System (TIMS) GIS database is accessed by ArcView GIS programs through Spatial Database Engine (SDE). The TIMS base mapping system developed for the Minerals Management Service produced the final customized plots.

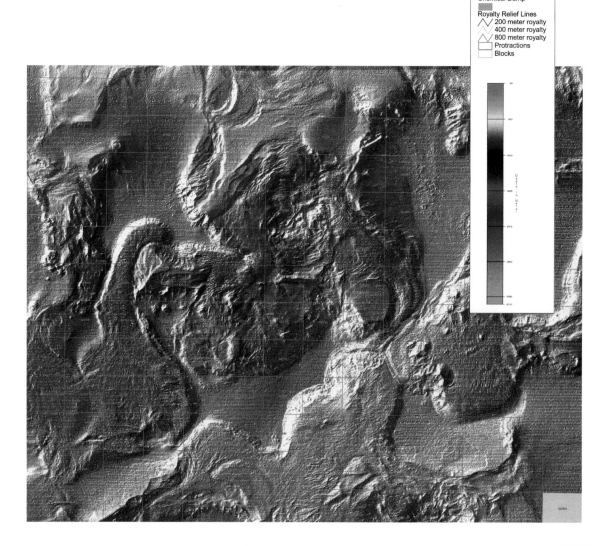

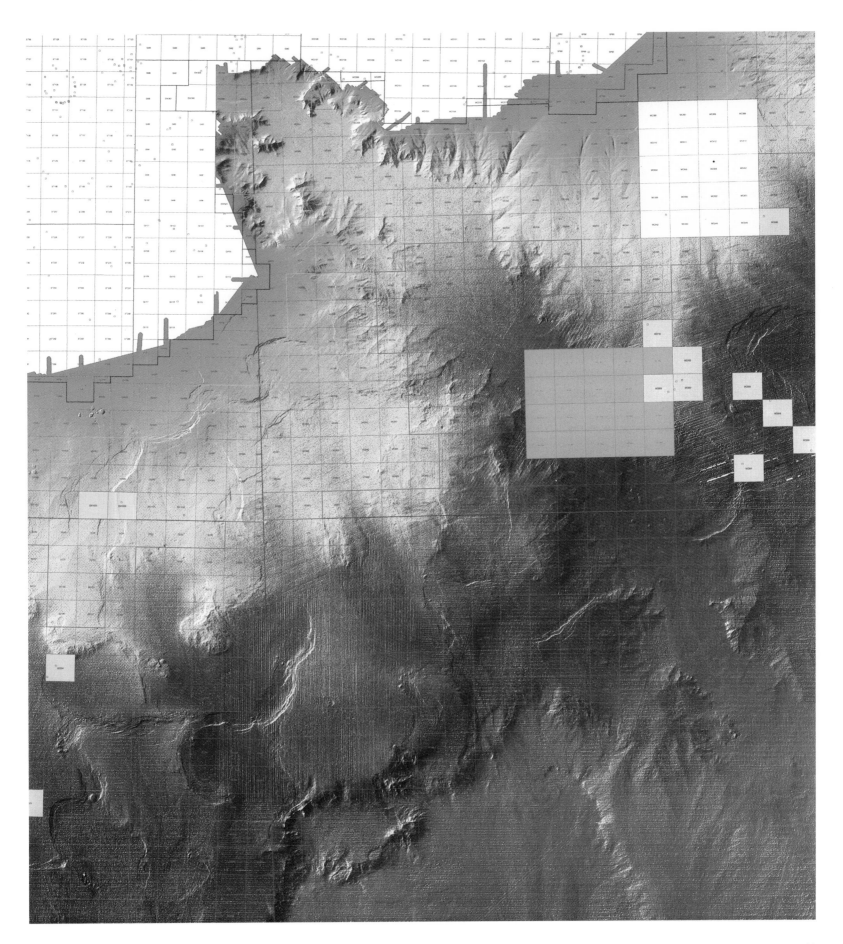

Using Customized ArcView GIS for Australia's Law of the Sea Project

Australian Geological Survey
Organization, Canberra,
Australia

By Robyn Gallagher,
Philip Symonds, and
Irina Borissova

Contact:
Philip Symonds,
psymonds@agso.gov.au

Software:
ArcView GIS and ARC/INFO
Hardware:
Sun workstations
Plotter:
Hewlett–Packard DesignJet 650 C
Data Source(s):
AGSO Surveys, AUSLIG, and
GEBCO

Under the 1982 United Nations Convention on the Law of the Sea (UNCLOS), Australia can claim sovereign rights over vast areas of its continental margin and adjacent ocean basins for seabed and water column exploration. Most of these areas lie within the 200-nautical-mile Australian Exclusive Economic Zone (AEEZ). However, in a number of areas around Australia, seabed jurisdiction is more complex.

The areas coming under Australia's "legal" Continental Shelf (CS) jurisdiction can be extended beyond the AEEZ provided they are justified according to the terms of UNCLOS. The Australian Geological Survey Organization (AGSO) implemented the Law of the Sea project to collect, analyze, and present data justifying Australia's claim for these areas.

The claim for each area of extended CS must be substantiated by bathymetric profiles across

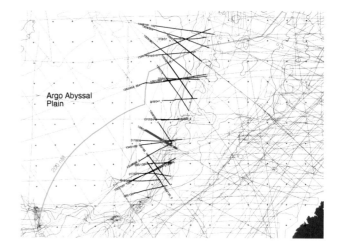

the continental slope. In many areas, an understanding of geological structure is important to support the claim, and seismic sections and/or gravity and magnetic profiles, satellite gravity images, and well data accompany bathymetric profiles.

A pilot study was set up to determine the best procedures for compilation, analysis, and presentation of the data and serve as a basis for studying other areas. The study produced a customized ArcView GIS for loading data and displaying profiles as well as a number of procedures using ARC/INFO.

Customizing ArcView GIS led to an integrated system in which profiles are automatically created for water depth and other geophysical parameters. At the same time, the program creates a line on the map corresponding to the profile. Survey information obtained from AGSO's OZMAR Oracle database is joined to the attribute table of the survey lines enabling queries regarding availability of geophysical data and navigational systems. Segments of survey lines are hot linked to the profiles.

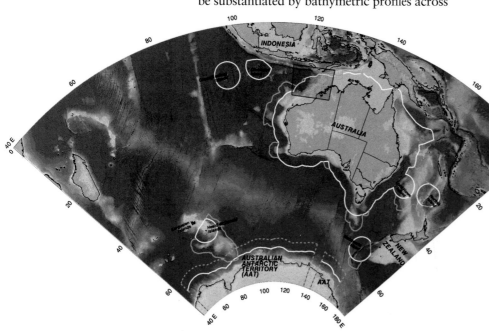

Australia's marine jurisdictional zones

GIS Applications to Maritime Boundary Definitions — International Diplomacy On and Under the Sea

MRJ Technology Solutions, Inc.,
Fairfax, Virginia

By Laura Crenshaw, Tracie Penman, and Lorin Pruett

Contact:
Laura Crenshaw
laura@mrj.com

Software:
ARC/INFO, ARCPLOT, and ArcView GIS
Hardware:
Digital UNIX workstations
Plotter:
Hewlett–Packard DesignJet 650
Data Source(s):
Multiple

Under evolving criteria established under the United Nations Convention on the Law of the Sea (UNCLOS), coastal nations continue to re-define their sovereign claims to ocean space. Construction of a global database incorporating both adjudicated and claimed maritime boundaries provides the basis for determining what marine activities are permissible under the UNCLOS articles. Graphic presentation of the location of such boundaries, along with attribute tables containing pertinent parameters, qualifications, and references to these limits, permits offshore operators as well as marine researchers to contact claimants in order to conduct activities that will not be in violation of either UNCLOS articles or the coastal nation's adjudicated claims.

MRJ Technology Solutions maintains a global database of maritime boundaries. It incorporates not only limits established through legal channels such as the International Court of Justice and coastal state's national tribunals, but also those claimed but not legally established or resolved. In the case of the latter, disputed or unresolved boundary claims are especially significant to mariners who may be uncertain as to whose waters they may occupy or transit. The database clearly displays areas of overlapping claims and questionable limits and while a disclaimer is necessary in such cases, attribute tables provide pertinent information on the nature and status of the claims.

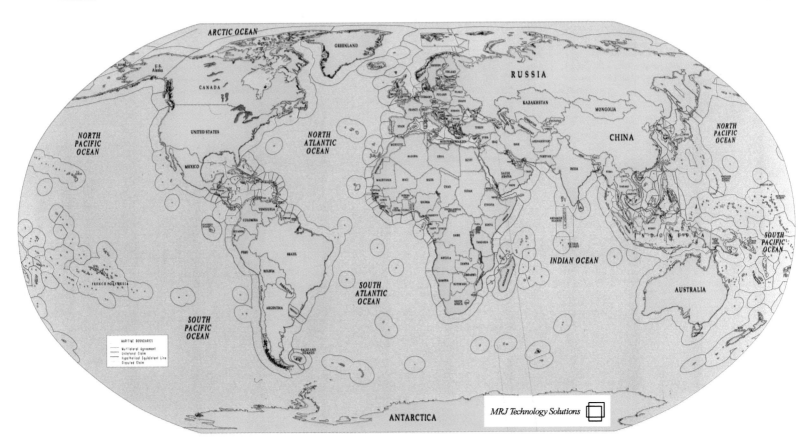

Lease Operators in the Northern Gulf of Mexico

PGS Reservoir, PGS Multi-Client, Houston, Texas

By Robert Arbo

Contact:
Robert Arbo
robert.arbo@pgs.com

Software:
ArcPress, ArcView GIS Version 3.0a, and ArcView Spatial Analyst
Hardware:
Windows NT
Plotter:
Hewlett–Packard 750C
Data Source(s):
Lexco Data Systems and MMS

This map is a visual representation of lease ownership in the Gulf of Mexico. It was created to give oil people a quicker way to view lease ownership. Subscriptions to updates of this map are available. Send an e-mail to gommaps@hstn.res.pgs.com for PGS GIS services.

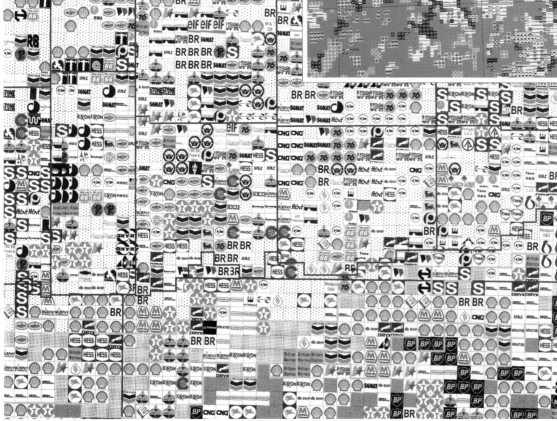

Petroleum

Movin' Out: The History of Outer Continental Shelf Oil and Gas Leasing and Production in the Gulf of Mexico

U.S. Department of the Interior,
Minerals Management Service,
Herndon, Virginia

*By Michelle Morin, Norman
Froomer, and James F. Bennett*

Contact:
James F. Bennett
jfbennett@mms.gov

Software:
ArcView GIS Version 3.0a and
ArcView 3D Analyst
Hardware:
Pentium 200/32 MB
Plotter:
Hewlett–Packard 750
Data Source(s):
U.S. Department of Interior,
Minerals Management Service,
Technical Information Manage-
ment System (TIMS), and NOAA
bathymetry

The oil and gas resources of the United States Outer Continental Shelf (OCS) in the Gulf of Mexico have contributed to fulfilling America's energy needs for several decades. A biennial record was created of leasing activity and production levels beginning in 1961 and ending in 1997.

These three-dimensional images depict the leasing activity for that period. The vertical gray bars represent barrels of oil equivalent (BOE) production levels for the year, and the green markers represent new leases for the year. This is displayed over Gulf of Mexico bathymetry.

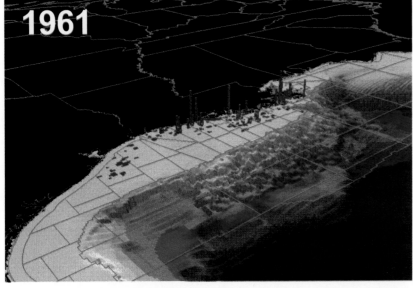

The Gulf of Mexico OCS provides approximately 1.4 billion BOE for domestic consumption each year and generates over $3.5 billion for the Federal Treasury. The single greatest production level for 1997 was 14.9 million BOE.

Improving technology has enabled explorations for oil and gas resources further offshore in deeper waters. The historical record reflects this trend. The Deepwater Royalty Relief Act of 1995 provides for suspensions of royalties to expedite exploration and development in water depths of 200 meters or more. Lease sales in recent years indicate the industry's willingness to accept the risks of exploration in these deeper waters. Successful exploration and production in deep waters in the Gulf of Mexico will help to fulfill America's energy needs for decades to come.

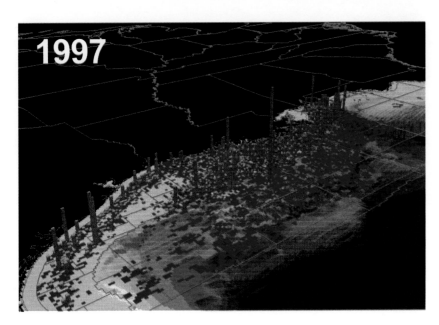

El Paso Energy Cartographic Productions

El Paso Energy, Houston, Texas

By Walter Kronenberger, Buddy Nagel, Gary Hoover, Shu Gultek, Domingo Llagostera, and Gary Witcher

Contact:
Gary Hoover
hooverg@epenergy.com

Software:
ARC/INFO Version 7.2.1, ARC GRID, ARC TIN, ARCPLOT, ARC NETWORK, ArcStorm, ArcView GIS Version 3.0a, ArcView 3D Analyst, ArcView Network Analyst, ArcView Spatial Analyst, and ArcPress

Hardware:
DEC Alpha 2100 server, DEC Alpha 400 workstation, Compaq 6000 and 5100 workstations

Plotter:
ENCAD NovaJet III, ENCAD NovaJet Pro, and Epson Stylus 3000

Data Source(s):
Business Location Research (BLR), MapSearch Services Inc., Wesson, ESRI, Minerals Management Service, Texas General Land Office, USGS, Tennessee Valley Authority, Teale Data Center, and U.S. Fish and Wildlife Service Central Division

El Paso Energy maintains a national-level mapping database with over 120 distinct thematic layers. These layers are spread across three ARC/INFO libraries, divided according to data density. The libraries are accessed by both ARC/INFO and ArcView GIS users. Prototyping on various designs was done to accommodate production functionality for ArcView GIS. The database is extensively annotated, with a goal to achieve publication quality cartographic display without relying solely on auto label in ArcView GIS or various ARCPLOT commands to generate labels during cartographic production. All libraries are maintained in geographic decimal degree coordinates to allow projection to desired parameters in ArcView GIS or ARC/INFO.

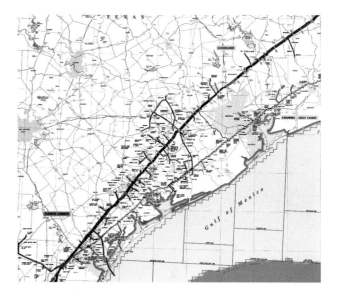

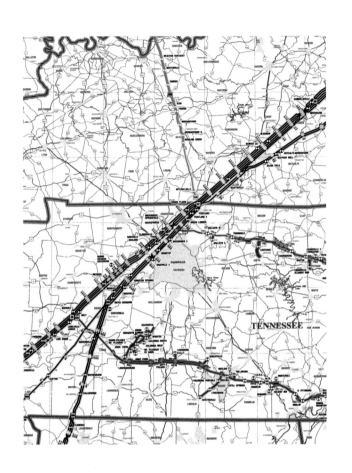

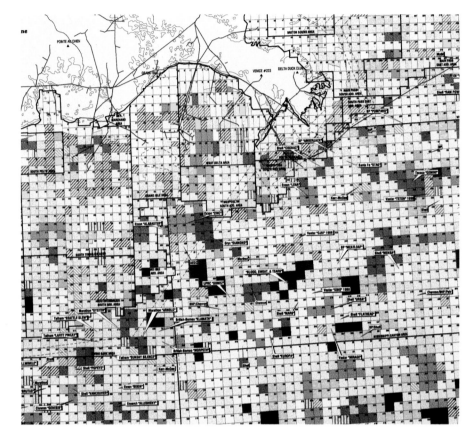

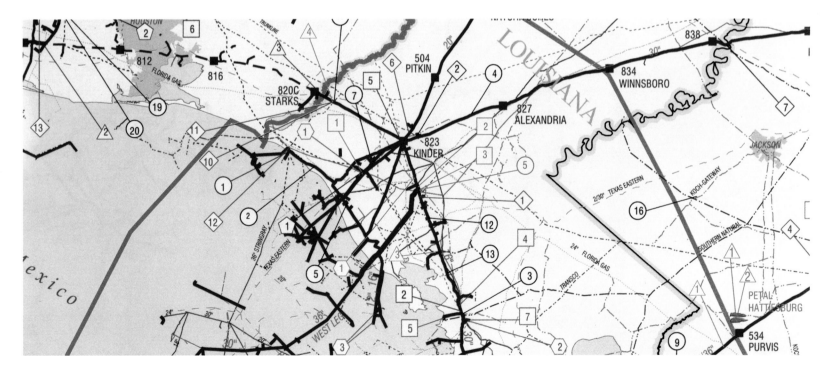

Northern Division Pipeline Map

Tennessee Gas Pipeline,
El Paso Energy, Houston, Texas

*By Walter Kronenberger,
Buddy Nagel, Gary Hoover,
Shu Gultek, Domingo
Llagostera, and Gary Witcher*

Contact:
Gary Hoover
hooverg@epenergy.com

Software:
ARC/INFO Version 7.2.1,
ARC GRID, ARC TIN,
ARCPLOT, AML,
ARC NETWORK, ArcStorm,
ArcView GIS Version 3.0a,
ArcView 3D Analyst, ArcView
Network Analyst, ArcView
Spatial Analyst, ARC/INFO
LIBRARIAN, and ArcPress

Hardware:
DEC Alpha 2100 server, DEC
Alpha 400 workstation, Compaq
6000 and 5100 workstations

Plotter:
ENCAD NovaJet III, ENCAD
NovaJet Pro, and Epson Stylus
3000

Data Source(s):
Business Location Research
(BLR), MapSearch Services Inc.,
Wesson, ESRI, Minerals
Management Service, Texas
General Land Office, USGS,
Tennessee Valley Authority,
Teale Data Center, and U.S. Fish
and Wildlife Service

The Northern Division maps are a series of three, which cover Tennessee Gas Pipeline's entire system division by division. The maps were composed in ARCPLOT using ARC Macro Language (AML) to record ARCPLOT commands. The marker set was customized with ARCPLOT, and the text set contains a variety of TrueType PostScript fonts. For a predictable appearance, a custom palette was developed by offset printing a variety of color shades. ARCPLOT line set tools were used to customize the line set.

The mapping database consists of ARC/INFO LIBRARIAN coverages, and the layers are extensively annotated for cartographic output. This helps in maintaining a consistent base mapping appearance throughout all products. Routes, annotation subclasses, text attributes, arcs, polygons, points, and regions are the feature classes used to create this map. All of the title boxes and graticules are automated using AML.

The continuous tone for the coastline was achieved using a line defined with many layers while increasing in width and percentages of cyan. Text masking was done during map composition by temporarily modifying text symbols to include a mask, with the text set to the same color as the mask.

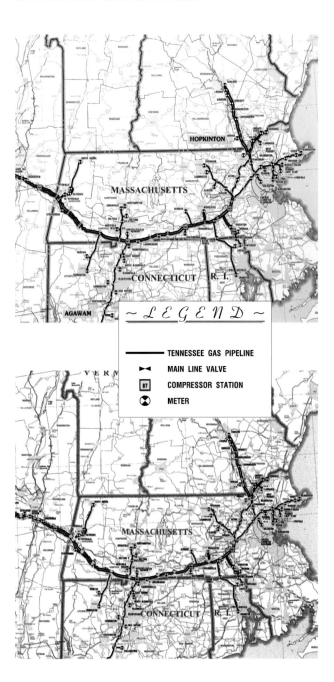

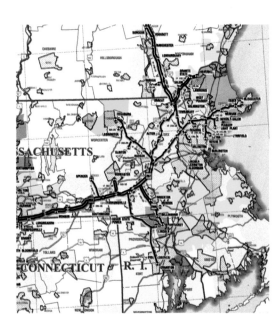

New England Area Infrastructure Map

El Paso Energy, Houston, Texas

By Walter Kronenberger, Buddy Nagel, Gary Hoover, Shu Gultek, Domingo Llagostera, and Gary Witcher

Contact:
Buddy Nagel
nagelb@epengery.com

Cartographic production and GIS analysis at El Paso Energy is as much a function of database design as it is a function of the tools to generate print-ready graphics. A "map-centric" approach to database design assists in achieving consistent, high-quality products with limited operator interaction.

ArcView GIS projects at El Paso Energy vary in scale and size of map, making customization difficult. Most projects are evaluated on a project basis, and previous projects will be considered when determining what themes are needed. Customization has been done to ensure color and symbol palettes are consistent from project to project. Scripts have been added to improve performance and functionality.

The New England Area Energy Infrastructure map was derived from an existing project and modified (additional scripts, themes, and tables). ArcView GIS projects consist of a combination of shapefiles and coverages. Text is placed using ARC/INFO annotation and label points from attribute data. Views are then added to the layout where title, scales, and legends are incorporated for completion.

Software:
ARC/INFO Version 7.2.1, ARC GRID, ARC TIN, ARC NETWORK, ArcStorm, ArcView GIS Version 3.0a, ArcView 3D Analyst, ArcView Network Analyst, ArcView Spatial Analyst, and ArcPress

Hardware:
DEC Alpha 2100 server, DEC Alpha 400 workstation, Compaq 6000 and 5100 workstations

Plotter:
ENCAD Novajet III, ENCAD NovaJet Pro, and Epson Stylus 3000

Data Source(s):
Business Location Research (BLR), MapSearch Services Inc., Wesson, ESRI, Minerals Management Service, Texas General Land Office, USGS, Tennessee Valley Authority, Teale Data Center, and U.S. Fish and Wildlife Service

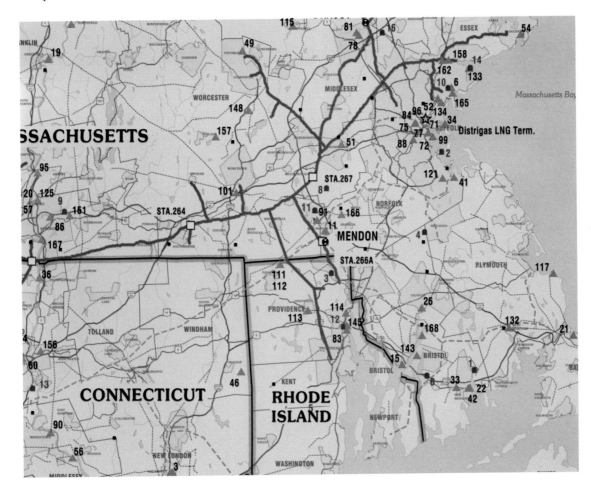

Using GIS to Plan the Communities of Tomorrow

Planning

EDAW, Inc., Irvine, California

By Richard Schwien

Contact:
Richard Schwien
schwienr@edaw.com

Software:
ARC/INFO Version 7.1.2,
ArcView GIS Version 3.0, and
ArcPress
Hardware:
Del-P 333
Plotter:
ENCAD NovaJet 50 Pro
Data Source(s):
EDAW, Inc. and Huitt–Zollars

Ladera is a meaningfully different master planned community of distinctive residential villages and human-scale neighborhoods. Social and recreational connections and innovative technology link these neighborhoods. Ladera will encompass several contiguous yet distinctive villages defined by factors such as thematic architectural styling and landscape character, product mix, topography, and major arterial roads. Each village will contain a signature social gathering place linked via a three-mile long lifestyle spine that runs the entire length of the community.

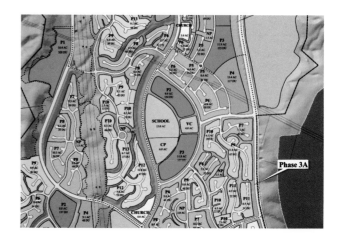

Maps for this project illustrate how GIS tools are used in master planned communities. Digital contours generated a relief of the proposed project and then were combined with the surrounding natural topography to build a composite grading model. The model is being studied and refined to create the new community of Ladera Ranch. Oblique perspectives were generated to see how the community would relate to the regional environment.

The product allocation plan illustrates what type of housing products can be built on the site. GIS tools enabled planners to easily alter the product type distribution, which changed many times during the planning process. Planners could then retrieve the results in tabular form for economic and financial analysis.

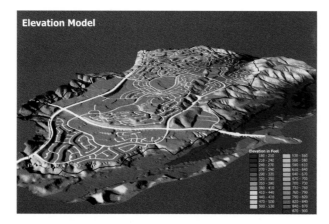

Elevation Model

LADERA RANCH

Redistricting with School Planner

The Omega Group, San Diego, California

By Talal Albagdadi and Merrilee Mitchell

Contact:
Talal Albagdadi
mail@theomegagroup.com

Software:
ArcView GIS Version 3.0a and School Planner
Hardware:
Pentium PC running Windows 95
Plotter:
Hewlett–Packard DesignJet 2500CP
Data Source(s):
Various commercial, local, government, and regional GIS sources

Due to rapid population growth and intense new construction, this school district's educational boundaries were no longer reflective of the needs of the community. The Omega Group was charged with developing a long-term plan that would enable further growth and improve transportation efficiency. School Planner was used to develop "what-if" scenarios, generate student reports, study the distribution of students, create ethnicity reports, and reconfigure boundaries.

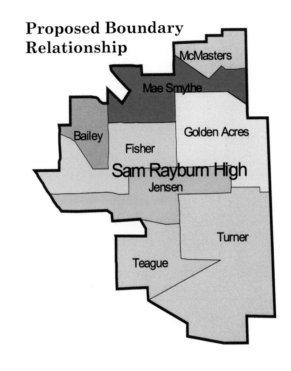

Proposed Boundary Relationship

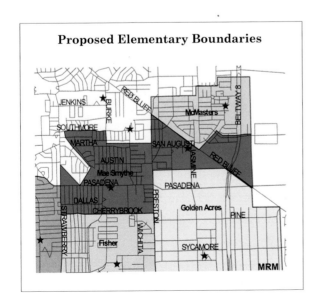

Existing Elementary Boundaries

Proposed Elementary Boundaries

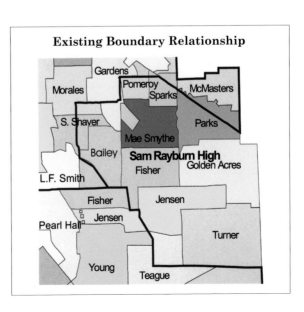

Existing Boundary Relationship

Lexington–Fayette Urban County Government (LFUCG) Land Use Map

Bluegrass Area Development District and Lexington–Fayette Urban County Government, Lexington, Kentucky

By Kent Anness, Rusty Anderson, Brian Mayfield, David Lucas, Shane New, and Phillip Stiefel

Contact:
Kent Anness
akanness@bgadd.org

Software:
ARC/INFO Version 7.1.2, ARCPLOT, and ArcView GIS
Hardware:
DEC AlphaStation 500/400 and Power Mac 9600/233
Plotter:
Hewlett–Packard 3500 CP/PS
Data Source(s):
Lexington–Fayette Urban County Government, Kentucky Natural Resources and Environmental Protection Cabinet, Bluegrass ADD, and field surveys of project area.

The GIS staffs at LFUCG and Bluegrass Area Development District cooperatively compiled the land use map using PVA and data sets from the LFUCG planning department. The map illustrates the community's land use plan for the next five- to 20-year planning period.

ARC/INFO was used to build the land use coverage from PVA and planning data sets. ARCPLOT AMLs were created to output the files to PostScript for post-processing and final map production on an Apple Macintosh. After a final review, the map was imaged to process-color film separated negatives at 2,400 dpi and printed. Copies of the map were included in the Comprehensive Plan text, and they are for sale to the public.

Sweetwater River Bikeway Use of GIS for Trails Planning

San Diego Association of Governments (SANDAG), San Diego, California

By Steve Kunkel

Contact:
Steve Kunkel
sku@sandag.cog.ca.us

Software:
ARC/INFO
Hardware:
Sun UNIX
Plotter:
Hewlett–Packard 750C
Data Source(s):
SANDAG

These maps illustrate some of the geographic layers in SANDAG's Regional Information System that are used for regional planning projects. They show the proposed Sweetwater River Bikeway and surrounding environment located approximately eight miles southeast of Centre City in San Diego.

The Regional Bike Route map shows the location of the proposed bikeway in relation to the existing bicycle routes in the southwestern portion of the region. The base map displays the surrounding communities and the local road network with parks, golf courses, and open space preserves. Other maps show topography, land use, vegetation, and sensitive species sightings. The digital orthophoto data displayed here was created through a local data development partnership managed by SANDAG in cooperation with the USGS.

This and other information in SANDAG's Regional Information System, including public land ownership; planned land use; historical and forecast traffic volumes; and historical, current, and forecast demographic information, are also used for many regional planning projects. For the proposed bikeway the public land ownership and land use information were mapped to determine what government agencies owned the land crossed by the path and where the bike path would cross private lands. Natural Vegetation and Sensitive Species maps display the impact on the natural environment. Demographic information can be tabulated for specified straight-line distances or travel distances or times from the proposed bikeway.

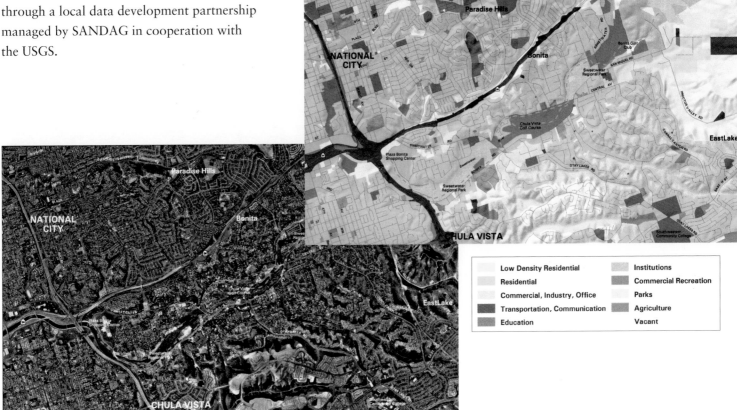

Low Density Residential	Institutions
Residential	Commercial Recreation
Commercial, Industry, Office	Parks
Transportation, Communication	Agriculture
Education	Vacant

City Master Plan Prague, Land Use Plan Proposal

City Development Authority,
Prague, Czech Republic

*By CDA Prague Urban Project
Team*

Contact:
Urban Project Team
uig@urhmp.cz

Software:
ARC/INFO Version 7.0.3
Hardware:
Sun UltraSPARC
Plotter:
Hewlett–Packard DesignJet
2500CP
Data Source(s):
Prague City Development
Authority and Institute of
Municipal Informatics of Capital
Prague

This map shows the Land Use Plan Proposal of Capital Prague. The land use plan uses two sets of criteria. The first set includes constraints on potential development due to natural, cultural, and historical factors. These restrictions were identified and taken into consideration in the plan.

The second set of criteria concerns influences on land uses resulting from a rising economy and increased population.

Delineation of the Areas That Will Be Flooded by the Birecik Reservoir and Site Selection for Resettlements

Republic of Turkey GAP
Regional Development
Administration, Ankara, Turkey

By Erturk Celenk, Ahmet Tumay,
Ali Fuat Cetin,
Ekrem Ozdegirmenci,
Gamze Arican, and Ilker Alan

Contact:
RS Geographic Information
Systems and Engineering Ltd. Co.
info@rsgis.com

Software:
ARC/INFO Version 7.0.3 and
ArcView GIS Version 3.0
Hardware:
Sun SPARCstation 2
Plotter:
Hewlett–Packard DesignJet 650C
Data Source(s):
Digitized data and digital
elevation model from General
Command of Mapping

The area covering Adiyaman, Batman, Diyarbakir, Gaziantep, Kilis, Mardin, Siirt, Sanliurfa, and Sirnak provinces in the southeastern Anatolia region of Turkey is known as the GAP Region.

Construction of the Birecik Dam, one of the GAP water resources development projects, is ongoing. Water storage in the reservoir will start in January 2000, which will flood an area of approximately 5,000 hectares covering 38 villages and the Halfeti town center.

A multi-disciplinary team (GIS specialists, economists, cartographers, geologists, sociologists, and city planners) coordinated by the GAP Regional Development Administration is identifying the environmental and socio-economic impacts of this event and will make recommendations. The United Nations Development Program is funding this project.

GIS was used for site selection for resettlements and to delineate the reservoir boundary. The reservoir boundary was overlaid with the ownership layer to determine the affected parcels and residential areas.

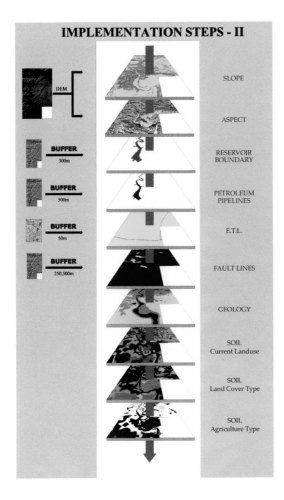

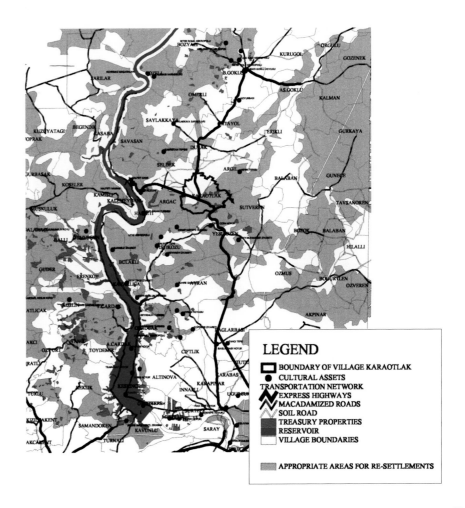

Telecommunications

CH2M HILL, Inc., Englewood, Colorado

By Daniel Moreno

Contact:
Daniel Moreno
dmoreno@ch2m.com

Software:
ARC/INFO Version 7.1.1 and ARCPLOT
Hardware:
Pentium Zoom GHz
Plotter:
Hewlett–Packard 755
Data Source(s):
Various

CH2M HILL, Inc., conducts facility planning and design projects for major telecommunications clients throughout the world. These projects range from high-level business and strategic planning to detailed engineering design, construction, and activation of broadband hybrid fiber optics cable systems.

Broadband cable technology is employed to deliver video, telephony, and high-speed Internet access to homes and businesses. ESRI software is frequently used to manage and analyze the vast amounts of land base, marketing, and engineering information vital to the execution of these projects. ESRI business partners throughout the world provide a ready source of information on local data sources.

For business planning projects on cable system upgrades in France and Penang, Malaysia, ARC/INFO databases were developed to examine demographic and land use patterns to estimate the number of homes served and revenue generation. This information was critical in evaluating the viability of the projects.

In Poland, potential long distance telephone services between major city pairs were estimated through application of weighted gravity models. In Spain, projected minutes of usage calculations were used to develop a backbone network for a proposed long distance telephone franchise. Broadband cable design projects in Spain and Malaysia required development of detailed land base information, including parcel boundaries and building footprints, to allow engineers to design and optimize the network.

In the future, the land base information will be tied to the engineered network to enable automated provisioning of services and outage management.

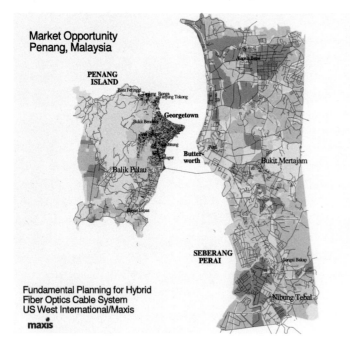

Market Opportunity
Penang, Malaysia

Fundamental Planning for Hybrid
Fiber Optics Cable System
US West International/Maxis
maxis

Cable Trunk Route Planning
Greenfield Development
Johor Bahru, Malaysia
US West International/Maxis

maxis

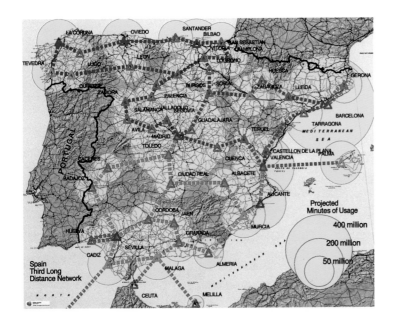

Spain
Third Long
Distance Network

Projected
Minutes of Usage

400 million

200 million

50 million

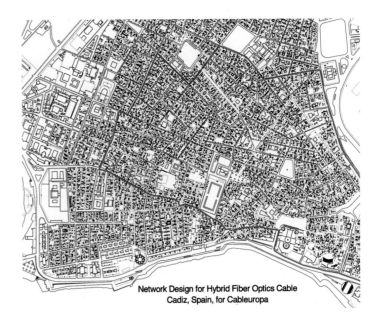

Network Design for Hybrid Fiber Optics Cable
Cadiz, Spain, for Cableuropa

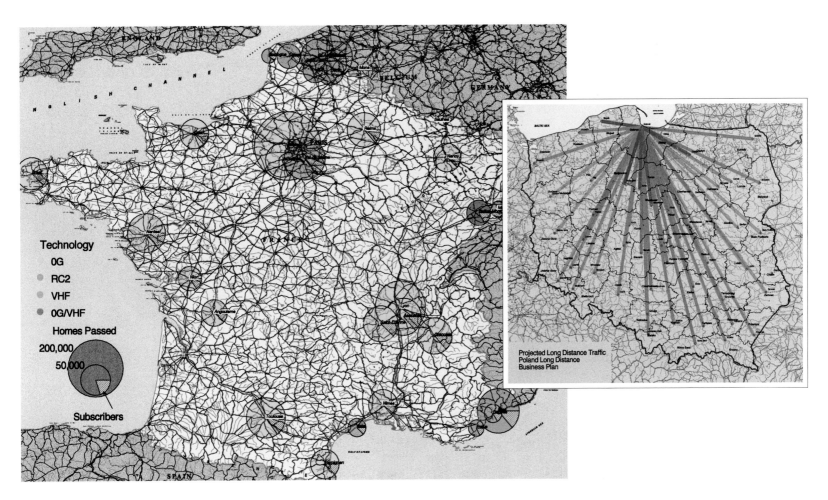

Technology

0G

RC2

VHF

0G/VHF

Homes Passed

200,000

50,000

Subscribers

Projected Long Distance Traffic
Poland Long Distance
Business Plan

Historic Frontier Trails Map of Johnson, Wyandotte, and Leavenworth Counties, Kansas, USA

Tourism

Johnson County Automated
Information Mapping System

*By T. Hensley, J. West, and
Sandy Wilkes*

Contact:
Jay Heermann
jay.heerman@jocoks.com

Software:
ARC/INFO Version 7.1.1 and
ARCPLOT
Hardware:
DEC Alpha UNIX and MacIntosh
Power PC
Plotter:
Hewlett–Packard 755
Data Source(s):
Johnson County, AIMS, and
Kansas City Area Historical
Trails Association

The cartography of the historic trails on this map is based on the original surveys done in 1854, 1855, and 1856 by federal surveyors. In preparation for statehood, these surveys, establishing range, townships, and section lines, were taken in Kansas Territory to conform to the Public Land Survey System of the United States.

Not only were the legal land points established, but the surveyors also noted natural features such as streams and rivers as well as the existing roads and trails at the points they crossed the section lines. The same system of legal sections exists today, and many main roads are actually section lines.

By the mid 1850s all of these trails had been well established. In some cases, there were earlier local variations of these routes, especially the Santa Fe Trail and Oregon Trail, but in the main, these were the routes as early travelers knew them. Great care was taken to follow both the maps and original field notes of the 1850 Kansas Territorial surveys, and they are the basis and authority for placement of these trail lines. In two instances, however, minor discrepancies were discovered in the original notes that required the discretion of modern cartographers of this map. In those cases, a dashed line indicates the modern cartographers' judgment of where the trail actually ran.

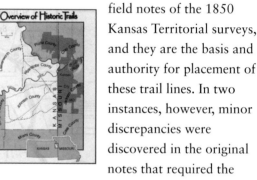

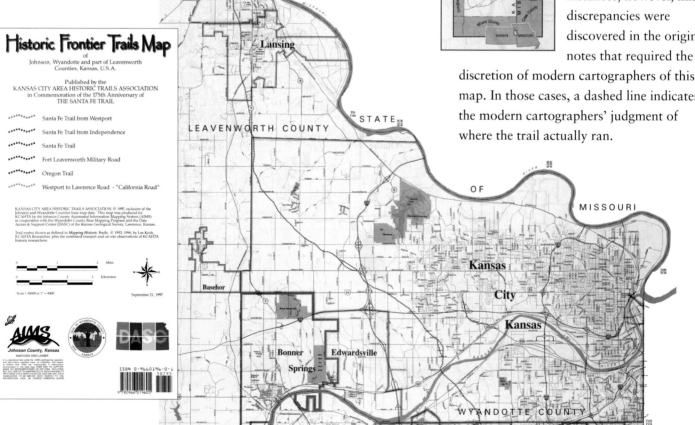

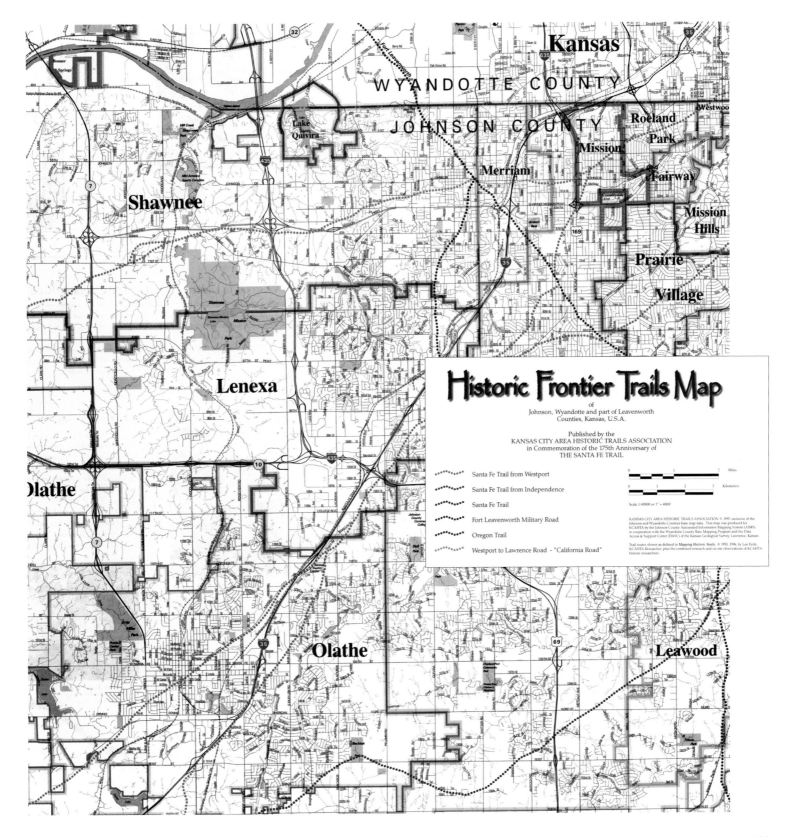

Historic Frontier Trails Map
of
Johnson, Wyandotte and part of Leavenworth
Counties, Kansas, U.S.A.

Published by the
KANSAS CITY AREA HISTORIC TRAILS ASSOCIATION
in Commemoration of the 175th Anniversary of
THE SANTA FE TRAIL

Santa Fe Trail from Westport

Santa Fe Trail from Independence

Santa Fe Trail

Fort Leavenworth Military Road

Oregon Trail

Westport to Lawrence Road - "California Road"

Transportation

San Diego Association of
Governments (SANDAG),
San Diego, California

By Bill McFarlane, Jeff Martin,
Sand Johnson, and
Andrew Abouna

Contact:
Andrew Abouna
aab@sandag.cog.ca.us

Software:
ARC/INFO Version 7.1.1,
ARCEDIT, and ARCPLOT
Hardware:
Sun UNIX
Plotter:
Hewlett–Packard DesignJet 650C
Data Source(s):
I-15 Major Investment Study

This map displays transit ridership and station boarding volumes by type that were forecast for the year 2015 for the I-15 Corridor Study/ Major Investment Study. This study is being conducted to help determine the best short- and long-term transit improvements for the I-15 corridor, between I-5 in metropolitan San Diego and SR-78 in northern San Diego County.

By graphically displaying ridership and boarding volumes using bandwidths and pie charts, transportation planners can easily review and compare the results of modeled transit alternatives. Planners must still review volume plots and reports for detailed information, but this map brings more dimension and meaning to the forecast output. This kind of map also saves time by helping to identify new solutions and when making presentations.

Since 1986, the San Diego Association of Governments (SANDAG) has integrated ESRI's ARC/INFO GIS software with the Urban Analysis Group (UAG) transportation planning software, TRANPLAN. SANDAG's use of GIS not only helps to display and better understand the transportation model output, but also assists in preparing necessary data inputs to the models.

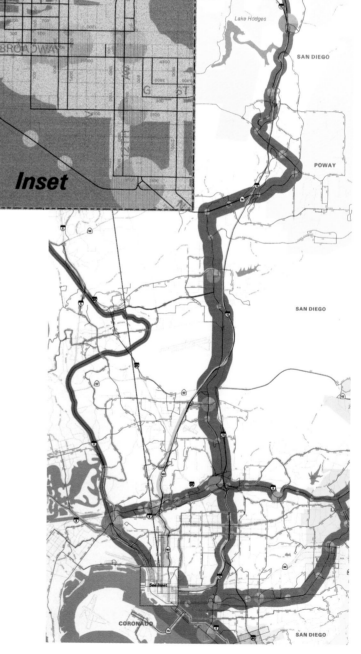

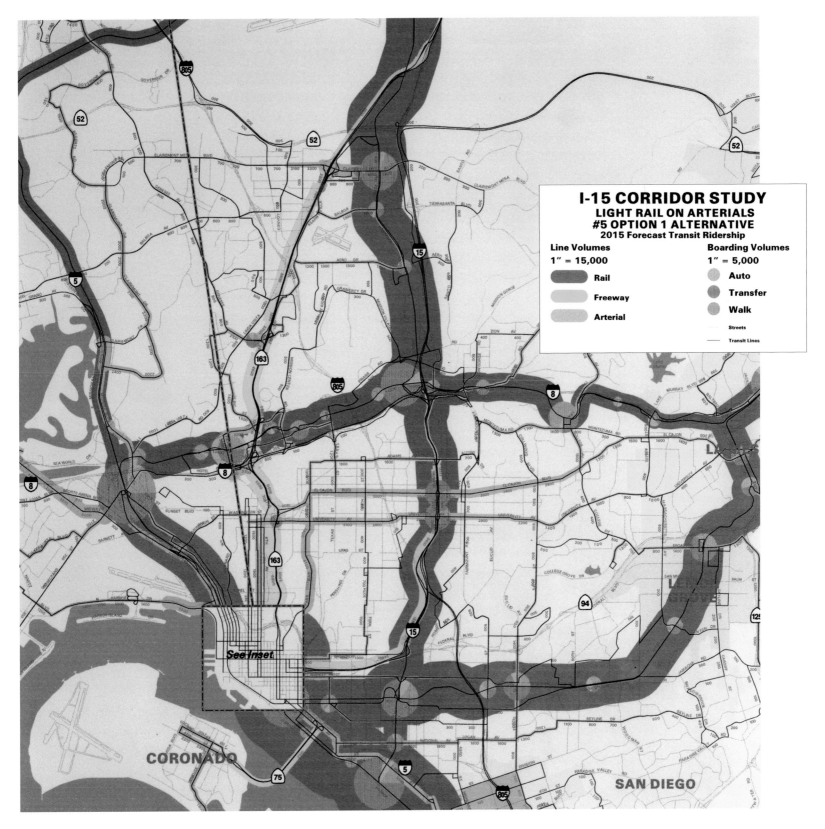

I-15 CORRIDOR STUDY
LIGHT RAIL ON ARTERIALS
#5 OPTION 1 ALTERNATIVE
2015 Forecast Transit Ridership

Line Volumes	Boarding Volumes
1" = 15,000	1" = 5,000

Rail
Freeway
Arterial

Auto
Transfer
Walk

Streets
Transit Lines

CORONADO

SAN DIEGO

Prepare for Take Off! GIS Proven Performance in Aviation Design

HNTB Corporation,
Kansas City, Missouri

By Jim West and Wade Frerichs

Contact:
Jim West
jwest@hntb.com

Software:
ARC/INFO Version 7.1.2 and
ArcView GIS Version 3.0a
Hardware:
Windows NT workstation
Plotter:
Hewlett–Packard 755CM
Data Source(s):
Proprietary

Tasked with the lighting and pavement design of select runways and taxiways at an international airport, HNTB used a combination of CAD, civil design, and GIS software. The result was a seamless exchange of relevant data among all work flow participants throughout the planning, design, and construction phases of the project.

GIS technology is used in aviation projects to quality control facility design and to produce dynamic maps and reports for construction management purposes. The client may incorporate the GIS into daily operations to create maps and reports and to document the lighting system.

The GIS illustrates two layers of data: aviation runway lights and sections of pavement. Additional layers of data, such as drainage utilities and terminal facilities, can be incorporated into the existing GIS. As layers are added, the GIS will represent more dynamic spatial changes.

Each time a new aviation facility is constructed, CAD files utilized during the design phase can be incorporated into the GIS. Depending on the type of CAD data, other aviation infrastructure management practices may include utilities, property and lease management, and equipment and pavement management.

The use of GIS for aviation applications will provide for a dynamic system in which geographic data can be spatially analyzed and queried.

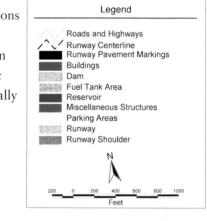

Figure 1: Spatial Analysis of Pavement Joints and Taxiway Lighting in Aviation Design

Federal Aviation Regulations for McCarran International Airport

Clark County Department of
Aviation, Las Vegas, Nevada

*By June Acosta, Kevin Graczyk,
and Dave Thompson*

Contact:
June Acosta
junea@mccarran.com

Software:
ARC/INFO, ArcView GIS, and
ArcPress
Hardware:
DEC Alpha, PC
Plotter:
Hewlett–Packard DesignJet 650C
Data Source(s):
McCarran International Airport

The airspace contours were developed from the rules set forth in federal aviation requirements and are plotted over elevation data compiled during orthophoto processing. By determining differences between airspace and surface elevations, height restrictions can be calculated for individual parcels. After adoption by the Clark County Commission, the maps will be part of an ordinance and public record. McCarran Airport planning staff, as well as Clark County planning and zoning departments, will use them to protect the airspace from intrusion.

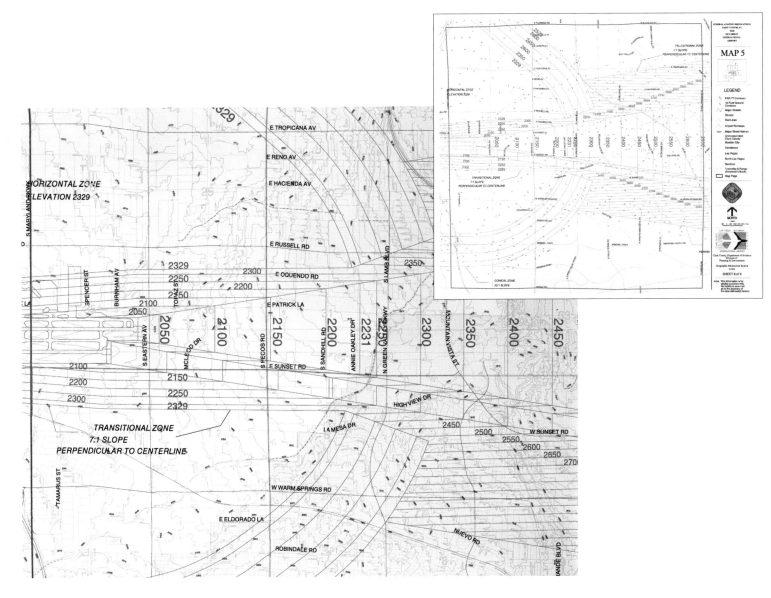

Georgia Highway and Transportation Map

Georgia Department of Transportation, Office of Information Services, Chamblee, Georgia

By C. Fleming, T. Leet, J. Martin, T. Christian, and G. Grant

Contact:
Tracey Leet
tracey.leet@dot.state.ga.us

Software:
ARC/INFO Version 7.1.2, ARCPLOT, ARC/INFO LIBRARIAN, and ARCEDIT
Hardware:
Digital UNIX workstation
Plotter:
Printed
Data Source(s):
Various

The Georgia Department of Transportation produces an Official Highway and Transportation Map annually. This version was the first produced using GIS. The statewide data was pulled from the county-level library (ARC/INFO LIBRARIAN) data.

The state routes and major connecting roads were pulled out and generalized, and data from outside Georgia was integrated into the GIS database. ARCEDIT was used for all editing, and the output was generated from ARCPLOT. A PostScript file for output was created, and the printer wrote films for the printing process. Recently, a newly created editing tool set has organized the data to make the files smaller.

This image is used as a backdrop for many special requests. ARC/INFO event mapping on county-level route data is displayed on this state map image.

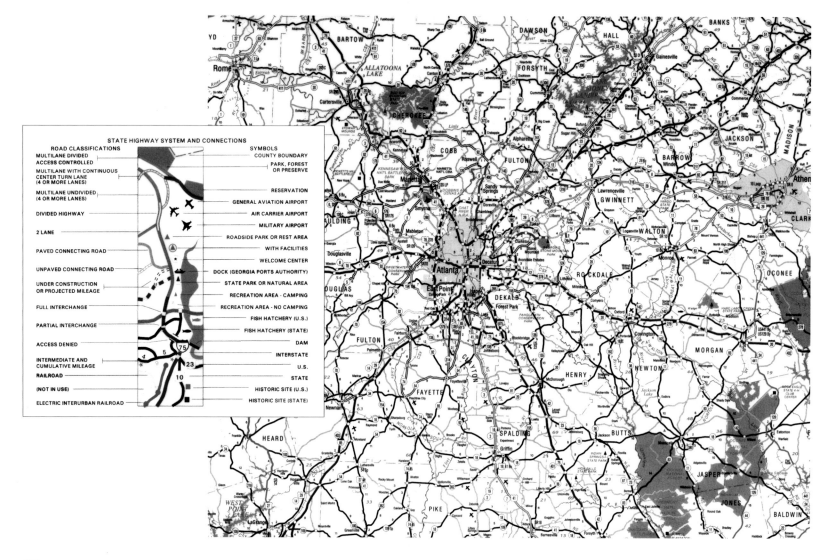

Atlanta Vicinity Map

AAA, Heathrow, Florida

By AAA Map Production Team

Contact:
Ramin Kalhor
rkalhor@national.aaa.com

Software:
ARC/INFO
Hardware:
Sun Ultra Enterprise 4000
Plotter:
Lehigh Press
Data Source(s):
AAA and Navigation
Technologies Corp.

AAA city and state maps are generated from a common, nationwide master database and projected on the fly for individual map products.

The master database is comprised of a collection of AAA proprietary and third party data integrated to form a comprehensive GIS database.

Based on the scale and purpose of each of the derived map products, a different set of extraction rules is applied during the development of each map. Various types of maps, such as country, regional, state, and city maps, contain varying levels of content and feature different specifications. In this environment, all changes and updates are performed on the master database level and are subsequently reflected in all derived paper and electronic products.

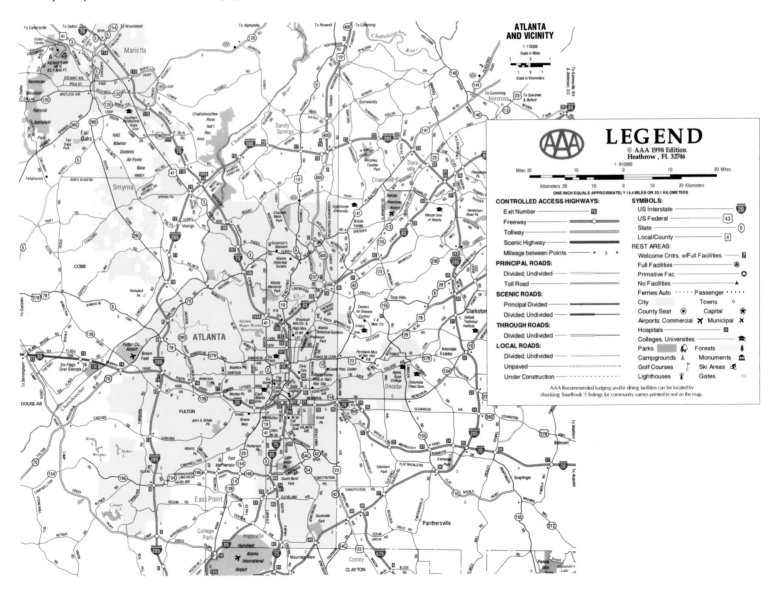

Regional Transit Map

Metropolitan Transit Development ment Board (MTDB), San Diego, California

By MTDB Marketing and Operations Departments, North County Transit District (NCTD) Marketing and Operations Departments, San Diego Association of Governments, Metropolitan Transit System, and NCTD bus and rail operators

Contact:
Judy Leitner
jleitner@mtdb.sdmts.com

Software:
ARC/INFO and ARCPLOT
Plotter:
Sheet-fed press (cymk)

 This cooperative effort between the MTDB and NCTD provides an overview of all public transit bus and rail routes in operation within the San Diego County area.

This complete map of San Diego County's public transportation system is distributed to riders. It includes schedules for trolleys, buses, and trains. Riders are able to use the same monthly passes on a variety of routes, transfer from one line to another, and get information from a central telephone center.

Travel Desires Between Municipalities and Doha

Planning Department, Ministry of Municipal Affairs and Agriculture, Doha, State of Qatar

By N. Balamohan and Rashid Saad Al Matwi

Contact:
N. Balamohan
nbala@gisqatar.org.qa

This map is part of the Travel Demand Analysis of Doha, Qatar, where more than three-fourths of the country's population is located. The analysis identified that the maximum number of trips generated was between Doha and Rayyan Municipality.

Municipal administrative boundary data (planning data) and population data (census data) were accessed through Qatar's GISNet. The travel demand data was derived from a 1995 origin–destination survey, adjusted by using emme/2 transportation planning software and imported into INFO Table. The key field of INFO Table was linked with the municipal data to obtain desire lines.

Trip ends of various land uses were extracted from an in-house application, Land Use Interface. The temporal pattern from the trip generation survey was used to determine the percentage distribution of trips during each hour of the day for major land use categories. Derived data was imported into INFO Table to get the activity pattern graph for each land use.

Software:
ARC/INFO Version 7.0.4 and ARCPLOT
Hardware:
Digital UNIX 4.0 and DEC Alpha 2100 server
Plotter:
Hewlett–Packard DesignJet 755C
Data Source(s):
GIS Unit of Planning Department, Central Statistical Organization GIS Unit, and PDP Transportation Planning Model

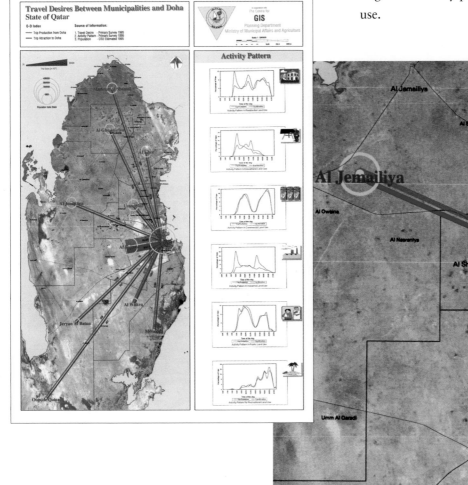

Urban Design Analysis

Rutgers University, New
Brunswick, New Jersey

*By Anak Agug Gde Agung,
Lyna Wiggins, Naveed Shad,
and Graciela Cavicchia*

Contact:
Anak Agung
agung@rci.rutgers.edu

Software:
ArcView GIS and ArcView 3D
Analyst
Hardware:
Windows NT
Plotter:
Hewlett–Packard DesignJet 650C
Data Source(s):
Sanborne, City of Bayonne,
City of Newark Department of
Engineering, and City of Newark
Assessor

 **Urban Design Analysis for Bayonne,
New Jersey**

As part of the requirements for a masters
degree, students in the Department of Urban
Planning and Policy Development at Rutgers
University must complete several studio
courses. During the 1997–98 academic year,
the students developed an urban design plan
for Bayonne, New Jersey.

Using Sanborne maps and other base maps
available from the city, students created a
variety of GIS layers for their analysis. They
found ArcView 3D Analyst a useful tool for
evaluating alternative designs. This graphic
shows an analysis used by one student team
to evaluate different designs for creating
"continuous greenways" through the city.
Building colors represent land uses.

Land Value in Newark, New Jersey
The map of three-dimensional building
footprints in Newark, New Jersey, is based
on the estimated building height. The building footprint layer and building description
data were provided by the city of Newark.
The map background is a 1995 digital
orthophoto from USGS.

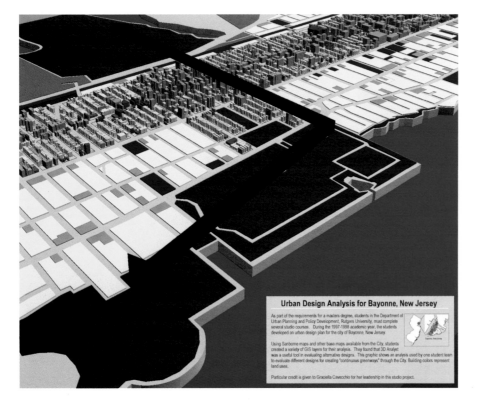

Urban Design Analysis for Bayonne, New Jersey

Land Value in Newark City, New Jersey

Massanutten Mountain in the Shenandoah Valley of Virginia with Modern and Historic Features Draped over a Terrain Model

James Madison University, Harrisonburg, Virginia

By Glen Gustafson and James Wilson

Contact:
Glen Gustafson
gustafgc@jmu.edu

Software:
ARC/INFO Version 7.2.1, ArcView GIS Version 3.0a, and ERDAS IMAGINE Version 8.3
Hardware:
Dell Pentium PC
Plotter:
Hewlett–Packard DesignJet
Data Source(s):
USGS, National Park Service, SPOT Image, and EOSAT Corp.

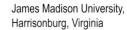

Merging a 1992 Landsat TM and SPOT panchromatic image with modern and historic vector data, these maps show the relationship between natural topography and Civil War battlefields and roads.

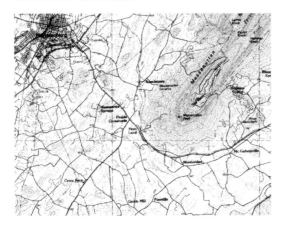
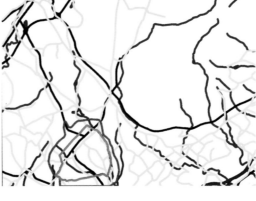
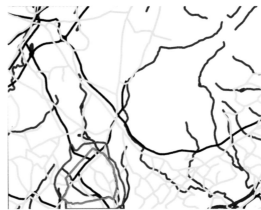

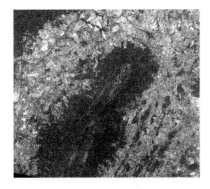
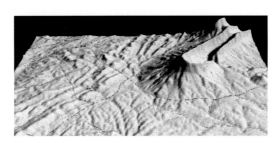
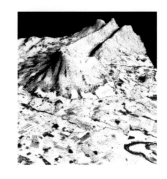

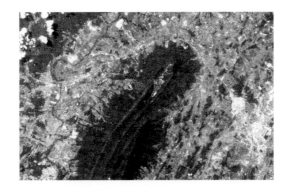
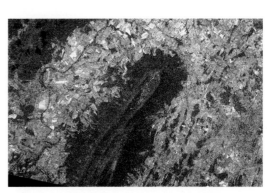

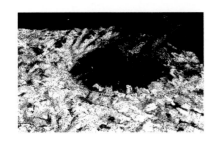

Sewer Flow Analysis System and Water Reclamation and Reuse Study

CH2M HILL,
Santa Ana, California

*By D. Bramwell, K. Martin, and
S. Lynch*

Contact:
D. Bramwell
dbramwel@ch2m.com

Software:
ARC/INFO Version 7.2.1
Hardware:
DEC Alpha UNIX
Plotter:
Hewlett–Packard DesignJet
2500CP
Data Source(s):
City of Honolulu, Honolulu
County, and public domain data

Sewer Flow Analysis System (SFAS) for Honolulu's Sewer System

The City and County of Honolulu have developed an innovative tool to plan and maintain the wastewater collection system—the Sewer Flow Analysis System (SFAS). It is a computer application that standardizes the city's wastewater flow modeling tools and procedures using a common data source in a GIS environment. The application will be used to assist the facility planning, design, and sewer connection permitting activities of the Wastewater Management Department.

SFAS uses state-of-the-art GIS technologies, hydraulic modeling, and data processing. The automated system provides a standard modeling platform for the city's flow modeling studies and links critical sewer capacity information to the Sewer Connection Application System (SCAS). The up-to-date flow and sewer capacity data generated by SFAS enables SCAS to perform over-the-counter sewer permit processing and approval.

Southern California Comprehensive Water Reclamation and Reuse Study

In 1993, the Bureau of Reclamation, with seven Southern California water agencies, and the California Department of Water Resources adopted a plan of study to evaluate the feasibility of a regional water reclamation plan. The study, the Southern California Comprehensive Water Reclamation and Reuse Study (SCCWRRS), used GIS to develop a model to evaluate various scenarios of promoting efficient use of water resources with increased use of reclaimed water.

An Allocation and Distribution Model (ADM), developed with GIS, helps identifying ways to maximize the reuse of reclaimed water in Southern California by evaluating alternative distribution scenarios and identify potential regional distribution systems. The GIS database, developed from public and private data sources for the region, includes base map data, transportation, hydrologic features, land use, terrain modeling, as well as reclaimed water supplies and demands.

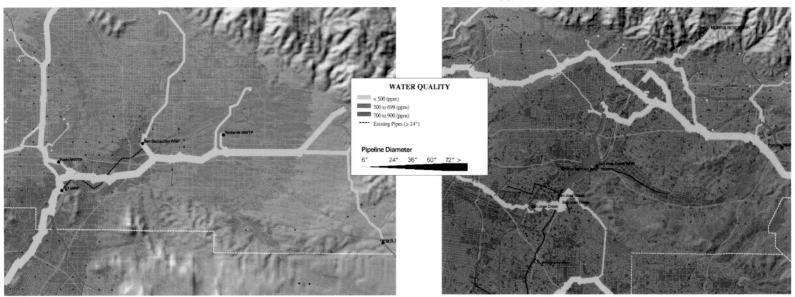

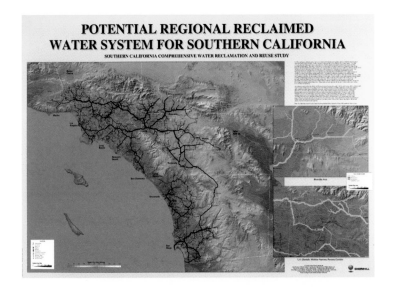

POTENTIAL REGIONAL RECLAIMED WATER SYSTEM FOR SOUTHERN CALIFORNIA

SOUTHERN CALIFORNIA COMPREHENSIVE WATER RECLAMATION AND REUSE STUDY

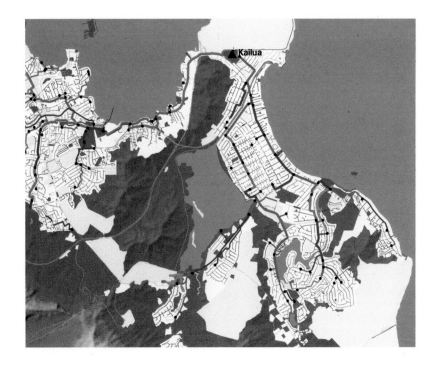

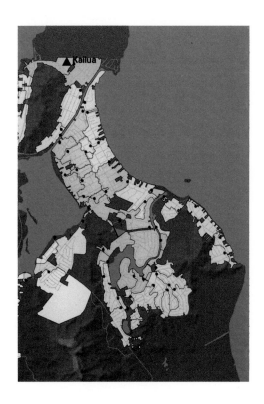

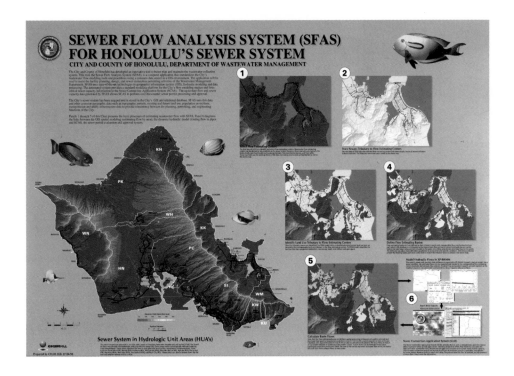

SEWER FLOW ANALYSIS SYSTEM (SFAS) FOR HONOLULU'S SEWER SYSTEM

CITY AND COUNTY OF HONOLULU, DEPARTMENT OF WASTEWATER MANAGEMENT

Sewer System in Hydrologic Unit Areas (HUA's)

Trenton Water Works Watershed Non-tidal Delaware River Basin

New Jersey Department of
Environmental Protection,
Trenton, New Jersey

*By Tom Atherholt, Gail Carter,
and Tom McKee*

Contact:
Tom Atherholt
atherho@dep.state.nj.us

Software:
ArcView GIS Version 3.0b and
ArcView Spatial Analyst
Hardware:
Dell Pentium mmx PC
(optiplex gxi)
Plotter:
Hewlett–Packard DesignJet 650C
Data Source(s):
NJ DEP and USGS

This map shows the watershed for the Trenton Water Works, which also represents the non-tidal portion of the Delaware River basin. Precipitation and air temperature were monitored at 15 indicated stations in this watershed as part of a study that examined the effect of rainfall on levels of two intestinal parasite microorganisms called Giardia and Cryptosporidium in the Delaware River. Other features, including roads, towns, and political boundaries, are for orientation purposes only.

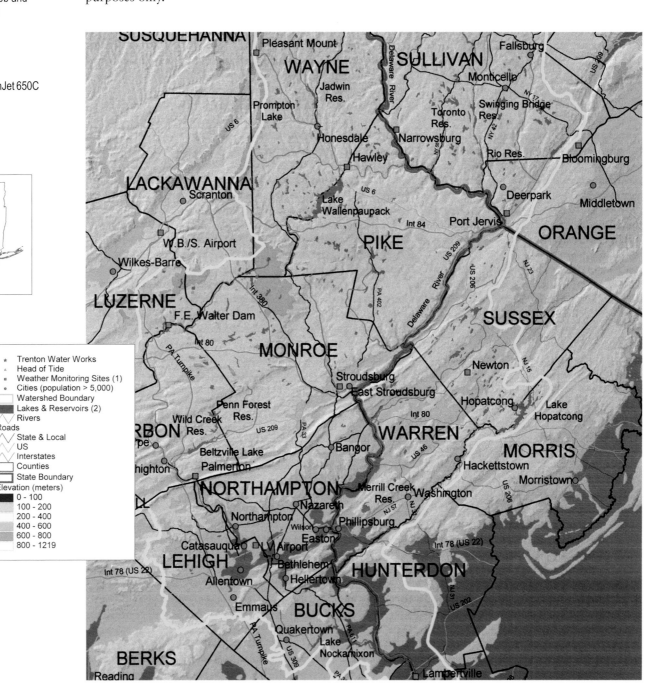

Cedar River Municipal Watershed

The Cedar River Municipal Watershed is a large natural area in the Cascade Mountains owned by the city of Seattle. It provides two-thirds of the drinking water for 1.4 million people in the Puget Sound region.

Cedar River Municipal
Watershed
Seattle Public Utilities,
Watershed Management
Division, Seattle, Washington

By Tom Van Buren

Contact:
Tom Van Buren
tom.vanburen@ci.seattle.was.us

Software:
ARC/INFO Version 7.2.1
Hardware:
Sun Microsystems
Plotter:
Hewlett–Packard 650C
Data Sources(s):
Washington Department of
Natural Resources, USGS, City
of Seattle, and King County,
Washington

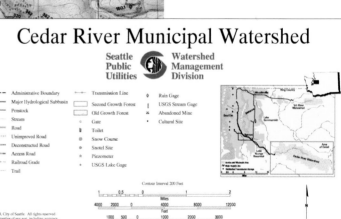

Sewer Traces in Jeffersontown, Kentucky

Louisville/Jefferson County
Metropolitan Sewer District,
Louisville, Kentucky

By Joe Wagner

Contact:
Joe Wagner
wagner@msdlouky.org

Software:
ArcView GIS
Hardware:
UNIX
Plotter:
Hewlett–Packard 750C
Data Source(s):
Louisville/Jefferson County
Information Consortium data

This map shows the sewer system of Jeffersontown, Kentucky, as well as the industrial users and companies with general permits that are located in Jeffersontown. The purpose of this map is to determine the location of key points in the sewer system and then develop a monitoring program that will assess the effectiveness of the pretreatment programs and, if need be, improve upon these programs.

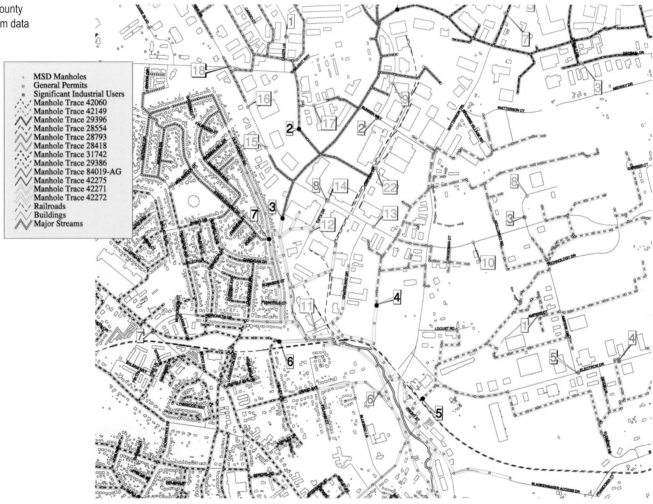

Geographical Analysis in Douglas County, Colorado

Douglas County, Colorado

By J. Alexander, G. Stere, S. Dunbar, L. Garcia, D. Kocheiser, K. Johnston, and A. Keeley

Contact:
A. Keeley
akeeley@du.edu

Software:
ARC/INFO Version 7.2.1
Hardware:
Hewlett–Packard 9000
Plotter:
Hewlett–Packard DesignJet 755CM
Data Source(s):
Douglas County Engineering Department, Douglas County Department of Planning and Community Development, USGS, Urban Drainage and Flood Control District, and USDA Soil Conservation Service

This map was prepared as a service to Douglas County, Colorado, officials for planning and regulation purposes. It is not intended to be used as a final judgment but as a guide for the decision making process. This product, along with field studies and detailed hydrologic reports of the area, can be used to define future conservation and development issues within the county.

The area depicted includes watersheds of Willow Creek, East Willow Creek, and Little Willow Creek. All three watersheds are located within a transitional zone, which occupies the area between the mountain foothills and eastern high plains regions in Douglas County. Running northward through the Little Willow Creek and Willow Creek watersheds is the Dakota Hogback, a geologic formation that creates a natural topographic and hydrologic boundary.

Sub-watershed boundaries were determined by the presence of existing development, bridges, roadways, and culverts, but primarily topography. The numbering system for sub-watersheds is consecutive from downstream to upstream along major drainages.

Streams were also numbered to effectively manage stream information, and the pattern used for the sub-watersheds was the same. Streams were numbered so that the last two digits correspond to the upstream design point (point of conveyance). Design point numbers were assigned the same number as the sub-watershed that is a direct tributary to each design point.

The numerous soil types present in the study area were grouped into three generalized categories.

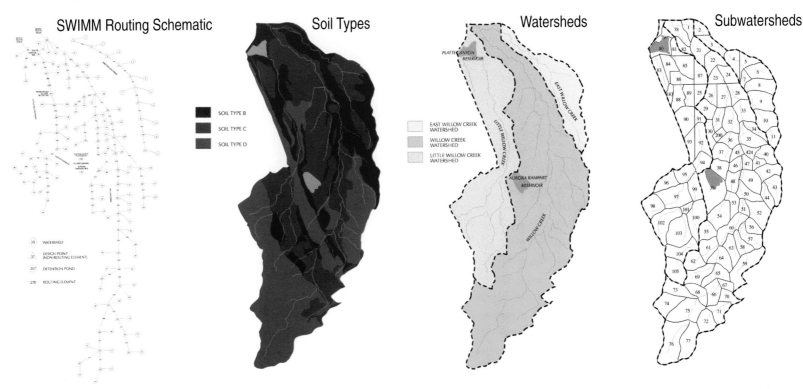

SWIMM Routing Schematic   Soil Types   Watersheds   Subwatersheds

Automatic Basin Delineation and Slope Calculation

Aeroterra S.A., Buenos Aires,
Argentina

*By Omar Baleani and
Adrian Benitez*

Contact:
Peter Barbero
info@aeroterra.com

Software:
ARC/INFO Version 7.1.2
Hardware:
Sun Ultra 30 workstation
Plotter:
Hewlett–Packard 2500C
Data Source(s):
Aeroterra

Automatic basin delineation, slope calculation, and other relevant physiographic parameters were determined within the framework of a flood hazard analysis for an oil extraction area in southern Argentina.

A digital elevation model (DEM), developed and owned by Aeroterra, was used to extract basin boundaries and various physiographic parameters using ARC/INFO.

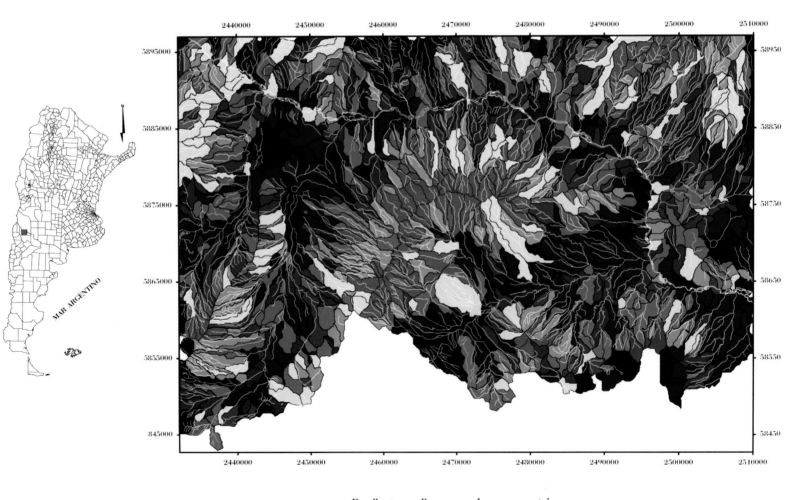

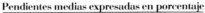
Pendientes medias expresadas en porcentaje

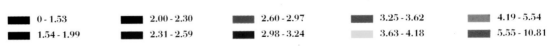

0 - 1.53	2.00 - 2.30	2.60 - 2.97	3.25 - 3.62	4.19 - 5.54
1.54 - 1.99	2.31 - 2.59	2.98 - 3.24	3.63 - 4.18	5.55 - 10.81